Critical Thinking for OCR AS Level T
Michael Haralambos and Rob Jo

Introduction

This publication contains suggested answers to the activities in Critical Thinking for OCR AS Level. The answers are *suggested* answers – to some extent, they reflect the opinions and priorities of those who have written them. In some cases, answers based on different perspectives may provide excellent alternatives to those of the authors.

The suggested answers are *selective* – authors have chosen to make certain points and include particular information. This does *not* mean that other points and information are irrelevant.

In many cases, the answers are longer than those expected from students. This is due to the addition of material to explain why the authors have chosen to give a particular answer. Often, background material is also included to provide context and aid understanding.

Using the Teachers' Guide The guide has a variety of uses. It can save you time – you don't have to work out the answers for yourself. In practice, however, many teachers like to amend and add to suggested answers, and put their own slant on them.

The guide can be photocopied for students:

✪ After they have completed an activity for comparison with their answers

✪ As a basis for class or group discussions

✪ For inclusion in their folders as a supplement to their notes and as an aid to revision

✪ As a basis for marking their own work – this may prove particularly useful for students on distance learning courses.

Acknowledgements

Cover and page design	John A. Collins and Tim Button
Graphic origination	Kevin O'Brien
Reader	Jackie Dickinson
Typing	Ingrid Hamer
Cover image	Getty Images

British Library Cataloguing in Publication Data
A catalogue record for this book is available from the British Library.

ISBN 1-4058-4941-X
ISBN 978-1-4058-4941-8

Pearson Education
Edinburgh Gate, Harlow, Essex CM20 2JE

© Michael Haralambos and Rob Jones

First impression 2006

Printed in Great Britain by Four Edge, Hockley

Contents

UNIT 2 Neutrality

Activity 1 *Neutrality and emblems (p13)*

Question 1 In order to do their work effectively, the Red Cross and the Red Crescent societies must be seen as completely neutral. If they are associated with particular religious organisations or particular countries, then they may not be seen as impartial and independent. They therefore need an emblem which reflects this neutrality.

To some extent, the symbol of the red cross reflects the Christian West, and the symbol of the red crescent reflects Islam and the Muslim world. In addition, the red Star of David, used by Israel, is a Jewish religious symbol. The proposed red crystal is not linked to any particular country or religion. As such, it is a neutral emblem and therefore appropriate to an organisation committed to helping people in need, whatever their religion, politics, ethnicity or nationality.

Question 2 Neutral sources, such as the Red Cross and Red Crescent societies, have high credibility. Neutrality means that they don't take sides, that they are impartial. They have no vested interest to lie or distort the truth. Because of this, their reports are seen as reliable and believable.

An emblem stands for and reflects an organisation. Since, the red crystal is not associated with any country or religion, it reinforces the view that the Red Cross and Red Crescent societies are neutral organisations. And this can only add to the credibility of their reports.

UNIT 3 Vested interest

Activity 1 *Conflicts of interest (p15)*

Question 1 Ian Campbell had a vested interest in maintaining the National Obesity Forum, an organisation which he founded to campaign against obesity. However, he also had a vested interest to campaign for effective methods to deal with obesity. In his view, the most effective method was prevention – to stop people gaining excess weight in the first place.

A conflict of interest occurred when, in his view, maintaining the National Obesity Forum in its present form conflicted with prevention. Ian Campbell believed that the Forum was so concerned with securing drug company money, it changed its policy to suit them. In doing so, it became 'too attached to "ineffective" medical methods for treating people once they became obese – including the administration of weight-loss drugs'. Since, in Campbell's view, this conflicted with prevention, he felt forced to resign from the Forum.

Question 2 Scientists have a vested interest in intellectual honesty. If they falsify their results, and this is discovered, then their reputation will suffer, they will be branded as a liar and a cheat, and they may well lose their job. Scientists also have a vested interest in career development and career advancement. Most want top jobs in top universities and the status and fame that a reputation as a leading scientist can bring.

In Sir Cyril Burt's case, these two vested interests may have come into conflict. Assuming that he did falsify his results, then he may have done so to protect his status and position as a leading educational psychologist. He was a major figure in his field and had been awarded a knighthood for his contribution to educational psychology. If the results of his research questioned his lifetime's work, then he had a vested interest in falsifying these results.

Activity 2 *Advertising cigarettes* (p16)

Question 1 Tobacco companies have a vested interest in promoting smoking and disguising its harmful effects. They are in business to make profits. And their employees, particularly the top executives, are concerned with defending their salaries and living standards.

Advertising helps to defend these vested interests. Product placement in films promotes particular brands and helps to create a positive image for cigarettes. Associating cigarettes with athletes and healthy young people and the 'great open spaces' also promotes a positive image. So does the suggestion that you'll 'feel your level best' when smoking – it 'picks you up when you're low' and 'calms you down when you're tense'. Further positive support for smoking is provided by stars endorsing cigarettes – Perry Como, an American crooner endorsing Chesterfield – and doctors giving support to particular brands – 'a medical specialist' recommending Chesterfield.

The positive images of cigarettes in advertising broadcast the view that smoking is a harmless and extremely enjoyable leisure activity. At times, they even suggest that smoking is beneficial – it increases your feeling of well-being. In this way, advertising has helped tobacco companies to defend their vested interest.

Question 2 There is no doubt that cigarette advertising distorted the truth. And there is little or no doubt that top executives in the 1960s and 1970s made a conscious decision to do this. As Fritz Gahagan (Item B) who worked as a marketing consultant for the tobacco industry states, 'The problem is, how do you sell death?' The answer is associating cigarettes in advertising with youth, vitality, health and fresh air. This is a clear distortion of the truth. The truth is that smoking is, in reality, associated with just the opposite – ill-health and death.

Activity 3 *Bernard Ebbers* (p17)

Bernard Ebbers had everything to lose – his company, his personal fortune and his reputation as one of the USA's top businessmen. If WorldCom's financial difficulties became public, his empire would come crashing down around him. He therefore had a vested interest to lie 'again and again and again'. It appears that, in desperation, he put a massive fraud into operation in a vain attempt to save WorldCom, his fortune and his reputation.

Activity 4 *Intelligence and spin (p18)*

Intelligence chiefs provide the following evidence of government spin.

First, the government 'passed off' material as official intelligence which did not come from the intelligence agencies MI5 and MI6. In particular, material from academic sources was 'mixed' with information from the intelligence agencies, and given an official stamp of approval. The intelligence chiefs saw this as a 'serious error'.

Second, reports from the intelligence agencies were 'doctored' to give the impression that Saddam Hussein was a greater threat than the agencies believed.

Third, the agencies were concerned about pressure from government ministers to find information to back the US claim that there was a link between al-Qaeda and Saddam Hussein. British intelligence reports did not support this link.

Overall, the intelligence chiefs imply the following. The British government wanted to invade Iraq and overthrow Saddam Hussein. They needed to justify this course of action. As a result, they had a vested interest in presenting Saddam Hussein as a much greater threat to the West than he actually was. This led to government spin and the distortion of intelligence reports.

UNIT 4 Bias

Activity 1 *Nazi Germany and Jews (pp19-20)*

Question 1 A prejudice is a pre-judgement which leads people to be for or against a particular argument, viewpoint or group of people. A pre-judgement means that a judgement has already been made *before* people encounter a particular instance of an argument, viewpoint or group. Racism is an example of prejudice – it pre-judges a particular group of people in a negative way.

Items A and B illustrate prejudice against Jews. *All* Jews are seen as 'subhuman'. This is clearly a negative pre-judgement. Prejudice often contains a strong emotional content – for example, a strong dislike or hatred of a group of people. This can be seen from Hitler's claims in *Mein Kampf*. For example, 'Was there any form of filth or crime without at least one Jew involved in it?' And it can also be seen in the cartoons and poster in Item B. Jews are portrayed as evil and subhuman.

Question 2 Prejudices are often irrational – they go against reason and ignore evidence which contradicts them. And they are often based on exaggeration and false claims. This can be seen from Items A and B. In Item A, the Jews are blamed for every major misfortune and problem of German society. This is an exaggeration, to say the least. And there is no evidence to support Hitler's view that the Jews caused inflation in the 1920s and unemployment in the 1930s. Prejudice dismisses contradictory evidence. For example, the Nazis ignored the fact that during World War 1, 100,000 German Jews fought and died alongside non-Jews in the German army. This hardly fits the claim that Jews were responsible for Germany's defeat in World War 1.

The cartoons and poster in Item B are based on prejudice rather than reason and evidence. As such, they are irrational. For example, there is no evidence to indicate that Jewish butchers made sausages out of rats.

Question 3 These are not credible sources for representing the Jewish people. They are based on prejudice. They are irrational. They ignore conflicting evidence. They provide no evidence to support their claims. They are an extreme source of bias which is based on distortion and lies.

Activity 2 *Reporting the Gulf War (pp20-21)*

Question 1 The language used in Items A and B clearly indicates bias. It is quite obvious whose side the writers are on. And it is quite obvious what the writers think of the Iraqis – they are 'mad dogs', 'brainwashed', 'cowardly' and 'ruthless', and their leader Saddam Hussein is 'demented', 'an evil tyrant' and 'a crackpot monster'. The language used not only indicates whose side the writers are on, it also contains a strong emotional component. The writers clearly despise the Iraqis and their leader.

Question 2 The bias contained in these examples may well reduce the credibility of reports on the war. It can be seen as understandable that the British media often took sides in the Gulf War. However, some of the words and phrases used to describe the Iraqis are so extreme that, for some readers and viewers, they probably reduced the credibility of reports on the war.

Activity 3 *Propaganda (p22)*

Question 1 Propaganda is an organised programme of publicity intended to spread a particular view and support a particular group. Propaganda is one-sided as it does not provide alternative views or give serious consideration to evidence which goes against the view it broadcasts.

The quote from Goebbels in Item A illustrates the one-sided nature of propaganda. His aim is to use the media to promote the government view and to 'instruct' and influence the masses. There is no room for alternative views. As noted in Section 4.3, newspapers which did not toe the government line were closed down.

Question 2 Assuming the evidence given by the Iraqis is credible, then it appears that the rescue of Private Lynch was a propaganda stunt, stage-managed by the US Special Forces for the folks back home. Governments often use propaganda during wars to present their armed forces in the best possible light and to raise the morale of the home audience. In this instance, US Special Forces are presented as brave and courageous, rescuing a helpless woman soldier who had been mistreated by the Iraqis. It's goodies (Americans) versus baddies (Iraqis) with the goodies coming out on top.

As this example suggests, propaganda is sometimes based on deception. As the Iraqi doctor said, the performance was like a fictional Hollywood movie. And it was just what the folks back home needed when American forces were bogged down with little sign of victory.

Activity 4 *World view as normal* (p23)

Question 1 *a)* In part, we interpret and judge the behaviour of others in terms of the culture of our society. Culture consists of values – ideas about right and wrong – and accepted ways of behaving. The interpretations and judgements made by Americans and Indians of the lawyer's behaviour in Item A reflect the values of their culture and their views of how people should behave. In this respect, their interpretations can be seen as biased – as favouring particular ways of behaving.

b) The term world view is used to describe how people see the world around them. Their world view is largely shaped by the culture of their society. People interpret events and judge the behaviour of others in terms of their world view. In this respect, the interpretations made by Americans and Indians of the event described in Item A can be seen as a reflection of their respective world views.

Question 2 In terms of the Yanomamo world view, the examples of behaviour described in Item B are perfectly normal and reasonable. And, in some cases, the behaviour is highly valued – it reflects the value they place on bravery and aggression, it brings respect and admiration to those who act in terms of these values.

Seen in terms of a British world view, the behaviour described in Item B would be interpreted very differently. Teaching children to admire violence and aggression, wife-beating, measuring a man's status in terms of his aggression, and fighting within and between villages would be condemned rather than valued. Blaming sickness and crop failure on enemies, and taking violent revenge for these misfortunes would be seen as senseless and stupid. And the death rate resulting from violent confrontation would be seen as a national disaster.

Activity 5 *Preferences and loyalties* (p24)

Question 1 Every person has their own preferences, opinions and views. In this respect we are all biased – we prefer one thing to another, we have our particular likes and dislikes, we have our own point of view. These factors will be reflected in your review of *Zoo* magazine. As a result, to some extent, your review will be biased.

Our preferences partly reflect our age and gender. For example, a 16 year old male will probably have different preferences than a 50 year old female. To some extent, these differences will be reflected in their views of *Zoo*, a magazine aimed at young males. For example, an older woman might find some of the illustrations offensive and many of the articles of little or no interest. In this respect, the reviews given by an older female and a young male can be seen as biased.

Question 2 *a)* Supporters of different teams have clear-cut loyalties, they take sides, and this will influence their reports on a match involving their team. In the example pictured in Item B, Pakistan supporters are likely to see their team's victory resulting from superior skills and tactics. On the other hand, England supporters may put their defeat down to bad luck, bad weather or bad umpiring. Some might even suggest that the best team lost.

b) The different reports may reflect the bias of the supporters. Since the Pakistan and England supporters have strong loyalties to their team, they will have a tendency to report their team's performance in the best possible light. As a result, their reports are likely to be biased in favour of their team and against the opposition.

Unit 5 Expertise

Activity 1 *Expertise (p27)*

Question 1 Here are the experts mentioned in the case study of New Orleans.

✪ Meteorologists (and hurricane experts)

✪ Civil and environmental engineers

✪ Epidemiologists

✪ Sociologists

✪ Professors of African-American studies and political economy and economics.

Question 2 *a)* The specialist knowledge and skills of all the above experts are relevant to our understanding of the disaster.

✪ Meteorologists, particularly those specialising in hurricanes, provide information about the weather patterns which led to the disaster.

✪ Civil and environmental engineers provide evidence about the levees and an explanation for their collapse, which led to the widespread flooding in New Orleans.

✪ Epidemiologists point to the health risks of polluted flood water which increased the death toll.

✪ Sociologists and experts in African-American studies explain why Blacks were the most vulnerable and the hardest hit section of New Orleans' population.

✪ And the professor of political economy gives a brief comment on the lack of government plans to evacuate New Orleans.

The combination of these specialist views provides an overall explanation of the disaster.

b) Had the government used the specialist information available from these experts, then the relief operation would have been much more effective.

First, had the predictions and warnings of the meteorologists been heeded, then preparations for the disaster could have been well underway before the hurricane struck.

Second, had the government listened to the concerns of the environmental and civil engineers, then they would have been aware that the levees were in danger of collapsing and widespread flooding was likely.

Third, had the government taken the advice of medical experts, then, at a minimum, medical supplies, clean drinking water and doctors would have been on hand in case of an emergency.

Fourth, research evidence from sociologists clearly showed the vulnerability of the poor, and particularly, low-income African Americans. With this knowledge, plans could have been in place to evacuate the poor.

Question 3 Experts have the knowledge on which to base predictions and give warnings. But, it is the job of local and national government to make decisions. As this case study shows, the experts were largely ignored until after the disaster occurred.

Experts operate in a social and political context. This can place limitations on the effective use of their expertise. Unless government officials listen to and act on the evidence and warnings given by experts, then their expertise is not being used effectively. Here are some examples of this failing from the case study.

The government had been warned by meteorologists to expect a category 5 hurricane. Their warnings fell on deaf ears. The government was totally unprepared for the disaster. Engineers had told the government that they needed increased funds to maintain the levees. Their requests were largely ignored.

These examples illustrate the social and political context in which experts operate. And they also show how this context can limit the effective use of expertise.

Activity 2 *Questioning expertise* (p28)

Expert sources are usually seen as credible. The previous activity suggested that relevant expertise was valuable for a) understanding the disaster in New Orleans and b) taking practical steps to deal with the disaster. However, it is important to question this positive view of relevant expertise.

✪ Experts often disagree – they can't all be right.

✪ Experts sometimes give incorrect judgements.

✪ Expertise can be harmful.

✪ The views of experts change over time.

The examples provided in this activity warn against unquestioning acceptance of expertise.

Item A argues that the medical profession is a 'major threat to health' because it directs attention away from the main factors which affect the health of the population – hygiene, diet etc. Item B provides some support for this view. It shows that the decline in the death rate from tuberculosis occurred well before effective medical intervention. This suggests that improvements in living standards accounted for this decline and that the effects of antibiotics and vaccination were relatively minor.

Items C and D question the credibility of the psychiatric profession. Samuel Cartwright's invention of the mental 'disease' which he called 'drapetomania' is plain nonsense. What could be more reasonable and psychologically healthy than a desire of slaves to escape from their masters? Cartwright's views simply reflect the prejudices and power structure of his day. From today's perspective, he is the person who is psychologically deranged, not the slaves he has diagnosed as mentally ill.

Many people would make similar criticisms of psychiatrists' views of homosexuality during the first 73 years of the 20th century. And many would see the treatment they gave to 'cure' gay people as little different from torture.

In 50 years time, as attitudes change, many so-called psychological disorders may be dismissed as a reflection of the prejudices of today's society.

The evidence in this activity suggests that expertise should always be questioned and treated with caution.

Unit 6 Reputation

Activity 1 *Nature and Bizarre (p30)*

Nature is the world's foremost scientific journal. Many of the most important breakthroughs in science have been announced in its pages. Its articles are peer reviewed – that is reviewed by experts in the area and returned to authors for improvement in the light of these reviews. As a result, *Nature* has a high reputation and high credibility.

Bizarre is a popular magazine which deals with the oddities and peculiarities of the natural and social world. It has a high sexual content as the cover illustrates – 'kinky sex with the women who wrestle men'. And it specialises in biological oddities such as the '3-legged hermaphrodite'. *Bizarre* aims to entertain, amuse, shock and titillate. It is not concerned about credibility. For example, in the issue pictured, an article entitled 'Retro Porn' has '100 years' worth of implausible stories' about sexual antics. This issue of *Bizarre* includes a free mini-mag full of 'Fun, games and sickening depravity'. In view of this summary of content, it is clear why *Bizarre* is not seen as a quality publication and why it has low credibility.

Activity 2 *Comparing newspapers (pp31-32)*

A comparison of the two reports in the quality dailies (Item A) with reports on the same subject matter in the tabloids (Item B) gives an indication of why the quality dailies have a higher reputation and more credibility. The *Guardian* gives a full page to the Denis Donaldson story. The report includes considerable detail and analysis, differing viewpoints, a historical perspective, and quotes from a number of sources. By comparison, the same story in the *Sun* is brief and shallow, it lacks detail and background, and contains only two short quotes from Donaldson.

The *Independent* devotes half a page to the Beatles' legal battle with their record company, EMI. As with the *Guardian* article, the report is detailed, it provides historical background and differing viewpoints, with quotes from both sides. The *Daily Express* deals with this story in two short paragraphs, tucked away in the bottom left-hand corner of a page largely devoted to Gordon Ramsay killing his children's pet turkeys for Christmas dinner. There is a short quote from one side of the dispute and hardly any analysis.

Compared to the quality dailies, the tabloids set out to entertain with celebrity gossip and human-interest stories – Elton John's marriage, Sara Cox's split from her husband, gossip from *Strictly Come Dancing*, and Gordon Ramsay killing the kids' turkeys for Christmas dinner.

The depth, detail, analysis, historical background, differing views and various quotations in the 'hard' news stories covered by the quality dailies give them a high reputation and high credibility. By comparison, tabloid coverage of 'hard' news is brief and shallow. The tabloids are far more concerned with entertainment and titillation and devote considerable space to human-interest stories and celebrity gossip. Hard news stories are usually considered more important and more significant than the 'entertainment' provided by the tabloids. As a result, the tabloids are generally considered to have a lower reputation and less credibility.

Activity 3 *BBC News and the nuclear debate (p33)*

Question 1 A balanced report gives various views on an issue. When those views are opposed, it outlines both views and gives the case for and against a particular course of action. An impartial report is a report that doesn't take sides and makes every effort to avoid bias.

The BBC report on the nuclear debate can be seen as balanced and impartial. Item A outlines the arguments for and against nuclear power. Item B compares two case studies – Finland, which is in favour of nuclear power, and Germany which has a nuclear-free policy. Spokespersons from each country are quoted. Item C compares the advantages and disadvantages of various sources of energy. On the BBC website, these are outlined in detail – lack of space prevents a summary of the pros and cons here.

Question 2 The BBC has a high reputation and its reports are usually seen as credible. This is largely because it strives for balance and impartiality. This is illustrated and exemplified in its report on nuclear energy. As outlined in the answer to Question 1, this report is balanced and impartial. As such, it can only add to the reputation and credibility of the BBC.

Activity 4 *Reporting the Palestinian/Israeli conflict (p34)*

Question 1 The evidence given in this activity is based on a systematic research project which analysed over 200 television news programmes during a two-year period. The evidence clearly indicates a pro-Israeli bias on BBC News. First, most reports were based on 'official Israeli perspectives'. Second, Israeli casualties were given greater emphasis, despite the fact that more Palestinians were killed in the conflict. Third, the language used to describe the Israeli and Palestinian killings was clearly biased against the Palestinians. On the basis of this research, BBC News was biased in favour of Israel.

Question 2 It is not possible to say, with any degree of certainty, whether BBC editors and journalists were aware of the existence of a pro-Israeli bias. The BBC Charter makes it clear that the BBC strives for balance and impartiality. It is possible that BBC editors and journalists were unaware of this bias. Many of the reports about the conflict came from Israeli sources. As a result, a pro-Israeli bias may have unknowingly filtered through into BBC broadcasts.

Activity 5 *Praising Aljazeera (p35)*

This unit began with the observation that the information provided by a source with a high reputation is likely to be seen as credible. However, we should not automatically accept that information is credible simply because the source has a high reputation. We should first ask whether that reputation is deserved.

If we take the word of President Bush and US Defence Secretary Donald Rumsfeld, then Aljazeera has an appalling reputation and its reports have no credibility whatsoever. For example, Rumsfeld claims its reports are full of lies and inaccuracies. Aljazeera has been condemned by many in the Bush administration as little more than a mouthpiece for al-Qaeda.

Should we accept this view of Aljazeera's reputation? Should we dismiss its broadcasts as lies and propaganda with no credibility? Judging by the items in this activity, the answer to both questions is no. The *Guardian* editorial in Item A sees Aljazeera as a 'pioneer of free expression'. It interviews Israelis and criticises Arab regimes, two firsts in Arab news broadcasts. The Index of Censorship in Item B praised Aljazeera for finding a way round censorship and 'contributing to the free exchange of information in the Arab world'. Add to these comments the positive views of Aljazeera outlined in the previous section, and it becomes clear that a strong case can be made that Aljazeera is a reputable broadcasting organisation with credible news reports.

Unit 7 Observation and eyewitness accounts

Activity 1 *Argument on a subway train* (p36)

The authors conclude that if an observation conflicts with what people expect to see, then their expectation may have a stronger influence on their perception and their memory of an event. The experiment supports this conclusion.

The picture shows a White man on a subway train holding a razor and pointing aggressively at a Black man. As the description of the picture was told and re-told, over half the participants stated that the Black man was holding the razor and threatening the White man. This made more sense to many of the participants because it fitted their expectations of the behaviour of Black men. In terms of the stereotype, Black males were violent, aggressive and hot-tempered. And, as the experiment shows, this stereotype shaped the perception and their memory of over half the participants.

Activity 2 *A bullfight* (p37)

Question 1 A regular fan would probably describe the strengths and weaknesses of the various bullfighters (matadors) and note the behaviour of the bulls – for example, whether they were particularly aggressive. They would express their approval when matadors made skilful moves and their disapproval when matadors were clumsy or the bulls were insufficiently aggressive. Regular fans would compare the performance of matadors with their previous performances and with the performances of other matadors.

Your account of your first visit to a bullfight would probably be very different. You may describe the setting, the behaviour of the fans, the costumes of the matadors, and details of the bullfight with little or no judgement about the strengths and weaknesses of the matadors. Your main judgement might be what you see as the cruelty of the so-called sport.

Question 2 An eyewitness account is partly shaped by prior knowledge. Most people who visit a bullfight for the first time have little knowledge of bullfighting. They will be largely ignorant of the rules and the various skills involved. They will know little or nothing about the careers and reputations of the matadors. And, in your case, when they come from a society with no tradition of bullfighting, they might see it as a cruel and vicious sport.

By comparison, a regular fan is involved in the sport, is aware of the rules, is able to judge the performance of the matadors in terms of the standards of the sport, and loves bullfighting.

As a result of these differences, the accounts provided by yourself and a regular fan would probably be very different.

Unit 8 Corroboration

Activity 1 *The extraterrestrial returns (p39)*

Rael's claim lacks credibility for the following reasons.

First, the evidence he gives is uncorroborated. No other human being witnessed the flying saucer, saw the ET, or heard what he or she said. The only person who could corroborate Rael's story is the ET who, apparently, has gone back to where he or she came from, never to return.

There is no evidence to corroborate the ET's claims. For example, there is no evidence of ET involvement with Buddha and Christ.

Second, the weight of evidence supports the view that Rael's claims are false. Apart from Rael's own claims and the small number of Raelians who believe him, the pieces of evidence he provides are so far-fetched that they suggest we should dismiss rather than accept his claims.

Weight of evidence for and against Rael's claims

For	Against
1 Rael's claim	1 Flying saucer
2 Raelian's beliefs	2 Existence of ET
	3 ET's ability to speak any language
	4 Earthlings descended from ETs
	5 ETs keeping a friendly eye on Earthlings
	6 Sending periodic messengers such as Buddha and Christ
	7 Rael appointed as final messenger
	8 Sensual meditation will save humanity

There is no evidence to support the eight points in the 'against' column. In fact, available evidence suggests they are all false. As a result, the weight of evidence is 8:2 in favour of the view that Rael's claims are false.

Third, the quality of evidence – its credibility – is low. For example, there is no evidence to support the claim that human beings are descended from ETs. The fossil record clearly shows the evolution of human beings and gives no indication whatsoever that we were suddenly created in the image of ETs. In addition, there is no evidence of a flying saucer landing in the woods in France or of a four-foot tall ET emerging from the spaceship and talking to Rael in fluent French.

Rael's claims are uncorroborated. The weight of evidence suggests they are false and the quality of evidence is extremely low. In view of this, Rael's claims lack credibility.

Activity 2 *GM foods (p41)*

Question 1 Both Monsanto and Greenpeace have a vested interest in promoting a one-sided view and selecting particular pieces of evidence to support that view.

Monsanto is the world's leading biotechnology company. It produces genetically modified food crops. Its aim is to make profits and to support its shareholders who have invested money in the company. For these reasons, it selects evidence to support GM crops.

The goal of Greenpeace is to protect the environment and biodiversity. They see GM crops as a major threat to this goal. As a result, they select evidence against GM crops.

Question 2 The National Centre for Biotechnology Education (NCBE) do not take sides on the GM foods debate. They evaluate both sides of the argument and attempt to present a balanced and impartial view. Given this, why do we need the views of Monsanto and Greenpeace?

First, it is useful to have a strongly argued case for and against an issue. By forcefully arguing from their particular point of view, Monsanto and Greenpeace provide a clear and sustained argument for and against GM foods.

Second, these two organisations may raise points and provide evidence which an impartial organisation may not have considered.

Third, the arguments and evidence presented by Monsanto and Greenpeace provide material for an impartial organisation, such as NCBE, to reach a balanced judgement.

For these reasons, it is useful to have the views of all three organisations in order to assess the credibility of the evidence for and against GM foods.

Question 3 Conflicting evidence can reduce the credibility of evidence. For example, evidence from Monsanto conflicts with evidence from Greenpeace, which leaves the 'person in the street' wondering who to believe, especially when both organisations have experts on their side.

However, this is not necessarily a bad thing. Issues such as GM foods are not clear-cut. Experts disagree. Evidence is conflicting. This is to be expected. Major issues always have evidence pointing in different directions and suggesting different courses of action. And it is no bad thing to question the credibility of evidence from all sides.

Unit 9 Selectivity and representativeness

Activity 1 *Unrepresentative samples (p42)*

Question 1 In order to provide credible evidence of the general public's views on fox hunting, a representative sample – a cross-section – of the general public must be selected. The readers of *Horse & Hound* will not provide a representative sample. First, they are likely to be in the higher-income bracket – as a result, members of the working class will be under-represented. Second, they are unlikely to represent the full range of views on fox hunting. As the title of the magazine suggests, it both covers and supports fox hunting. Used as evidence of the general public's views on fox hunting, the results of a questionnaire in *Horse & Hound* have low credibility.

Question 2 Using voting intentions to predict the results of a forthcoming general election requires a representative sample of the population eligible to vote. Readers of *Woman's Own* will not provide a representative sample of this population. First, the vast majority of readers are women. Second, they tend to be older women. In terms of gender and age, the sample will be unrepresentative.

Question 3 The readership of *Sugar* consists primarily of teenage girls. In this respect, the questionnaire may reflect young people's attitudes. However, it will not reflect the attitudes of male teenagers. As with other magazines, the readership of *Sugar* does not provide a representative sample of the population that is being investigated.

Activity 2 *Unrepresentative reporting (p44)*

Question 1 Judging from the research outlined in Item B, the picture on the right is typical of the strike. According to those who were there, both striking miners and the police spent most of their time standing round and doing nothing.

Question 2 Reports of police and striking miners standing round and doing nothing are not considered 'newsworthy'. On the other hand, violent confrontations are much more likely to be seen by editors and journalists as suitable for inclusion in TV news. They are seen as more significant and interesting. Violence breaks the law and lawbreaking is a standard part of news reporting. Violent confrontations can provide compelling viewing – they are active rather than passive, they involve strong emotions and they can shock the viewer.

Question 3 This activity points to the dangers of selection. TV news did not present a balanced report of the miners' strike. Instead, it focused on violent clashes between picketing miners and the police. Such incidents were not typical of the strike. However, those who had no direct knowledge of the strike relied on media reports and believed that the picketing was mostly violent. In this respect, it can be argued that they were misinformed, that they had been given a false impression of the strike.

This is a serious criticism of TV news. Clearly, the news media have to select – they cannot cover everything. However, selection should not misrepresent – it should present a balanced report of events. In the case of the miners' strike, TV news failed to reflect what actually happened.

Activity 3 *Reporting crime statistics (p45)*

Question 1 The report by the *Daily Mail* focuses almost exclusively on violent crime. This focus can be seen from its headline, 'In a single year, more than a million victims are attacked'. The *Mail* rejects the figures from the British Crime Survey, which indicate an 11% fall in violent crime, despite the fact that it is generally regarded as the most reliable indicator of crime trends. And the *Mail* ignores the possibility, reported in the *Guardian*, that the rise in violent crime indicated by police recorded crime may be due to 'recording practices and targeted initiatives' rather than an actual rise.

Clearly the *Mail* has selected evidence which supports its campaign against violent crime and ignored or rejected evidence which questions its claim that there has been a rapid rise in violent crime.

Question 2 *a)* The language and tone of the *Guardian* report are restrained and unemotional. The same applies to the quotations used in the report. The language and tone of the *Daily Mail* report are less restrained and more emotional with phrases like 'the pain and fear of violent attack' which are designed to appeal to the emotions. The quote from Shadow Home Secretary David Davis which states that violent crime is 'continuing to spiral out of control' tends to sensationalise the issue. The *Mail* is clearly in a combative mood when it attacks Tony Blair and the Labour Party.

b) The language and tone of the *Guardian* article suggest that it is not taking sides. There is no indication of bias. The tone of the *Mail's* report suggests that it is continuing its campaign against violent crime. It is critical of government policy and singles out Tony Blair for blame. The language used suggests that the report is biased rather than impartial.

Question 3 The *Guardian* report is more credible for the following reasons.

First, it gives an overall picture of the range of crime from two sources – the British Crime Survey and police recorded crime. By comparison, the *Mail* relies heavily on police recorded crime statistics and dismisses the British Crime Survey results. In addition, the *Mail* focuses on violent crime and has little to say about other changes in the crime rate.

Second, the *Guardian* quotes experts who comment on the British Crime Survey and police recorded crime statistics. These quotes help to explain the differing figures on violent crime from these sources. By comparison the *Mail* quotes David Davis who appears to be either playing politics or to be completely ignorant of the British Crime Survey results and the real possibility that police recorded crime statistics may indicate an apparent but *not* an actual rise in violent crime.

Third, the *Mail* report contains inaccuracies. For example, the then Home Secretary, Charles Clarke, was not under pressure from Tony Blair to publish the results of the British Crime Survey. The survey is conducted every year and the results are regularly published by the Home Office along with the annual police recorded crime statistics. The publication of the British Crime Survey results is standard practice, not the result of pressure from the Prime Minister.

The above reasons suggest that the *Guardian* provides a more credible report than the *Daily Mail*.

Unit 10 Context

Activity 1 *The Reichstag fire (p47)*

Question 1 When the police investigate a case of suspected arson, they often begin by asking who had a motive for deliberately setting fire to the building. In the case of the Reichstag fire, the historical context is essential in order to investigate possible motives. Without information about the political situation in Nazi Germany during the early 1930s, it would not be possible to assess the various claims about who started the fire.

A brief survey of the historical context shows that both the Nazis and those who opposed them may have had a motive for setting fire to the Reichstag. For example, it gave Hitler and the Nazis the excuse they needed to tighten their grip on power.

Question 2 This is a difficult question to answer. The historical context provides some credibility for evidence which points to each of the suspected individuals and groups. Even today, historians are still arguing about who started the Reichstag fire.

Activity 2 *Science in context (p48)*

Assessing the credibility of evidence always takes place within a context – within a particular social context and during a particular time period. It is essential to recognise this when assessing the credibility of evidence. Clearly, the beliefs and values of the context will affect assessment of credibility – especially when the evidence challenges those beliefs and values. Galileo's experience illustrates this point.

Today, practically everybody agrees with Galileo that the Earth orbits the Sun. However, when he made this claim and presented evidence to support it, his views were rejected by Italy's leading scholars and churchmen. Galileo had challenged the accepted view that the Earth was the centre of the universe. He had called into question the beliefs of the leading scholars of the day – astronomers, mathematicians and philosophers. They were not going to surrender their beliefs without a fight. And Galileo's claims contradicted the teachings of the Roman Catholic Church. The leading churchmen were not about to change what they saw as the word of God. As a result of this widespread opposition, Galileo's views were given no credibility and rejected.

Charles Darwin had a somewhat easier time when he announced his theory of evolution by natural selection. However, he too was condemned by many members of the scientific establishment and religious leaders. In addition, he was ridiculed in the popular press. Today, Darwin's ideas form the basis of the biological sciences. However, they are still opposed by some religious groups.

What can we learn from these examples? First, each and every one of us assesses evidence within a social context and within a particular time period. We are inevitably influenced by these factors. And it is essential to realise this.

When assessing the credibility of evidence, is our judgement unduly influenced if that evidence challenges our beliefs and values? Do we reject evidence simply because it contradicts our religious beliefs? Do we dismiss evidence because it threatens our position, status and beliefs as a scientist, doctor, civil engineer and so on? Do we regard evidence as unbelievable because it seems far-fetched in terms of today's perspectives? These are questions we must seriously consider when assessing the credibility of evidence.

Activity 3 *Two interviews (p49)*

A considerable amount of evidence comes from question and answer sessions – for example, from interviews by researchers and journalists. Interviews take place in social contexts. As the two interviews in this activity show, the context can shape the responses of the interviewee.

In the first interview, the boy's responses are minimal – long silences and two or three word answers. Clearly, the boy is ill at ease in this formal setting.

In the second interview the context is changed. The setting is now informal – the interviewer sits on the floor, the boy is provided with a supply of crisps and joined by his best friend. The boy is now relaxed and at ease. The change is dramatic – the conversation flows and the boy gives detailed answers.

The comparison between the two interviews shows the importance of context. Different contexts can produce very different responses. Clearly, context must be taken into account when assessing the credibility of interview data.

Activity 4 *Changing the verb (p50)*

Question 1 Each group watched the same film. Each group was asked the same question apart from a change in a single word – the verb. The three different verbs suggested that the force of the impact was different in each case. And this, in turn, suggested that the cars were going at different speeds when they collided. As a result, the estimates given by each group differed.

Question 2 This example shows the importance of the linguistic context. It shows how particular words and phrases can affect the responses people give in conversations or in interview situations. When assessing the credibility of this type of data, it is important to be aware of the possible effects of the linguistic context.

Unit 11 Sources and types of evidence

Activity 1 Re-writing history (p52)

Question 1 Lenin was one of the founders of the Soviet Union. He was highly respected as the founding father of the Soviet state. Leaders associated with Lenin shared this respect. This is probably why Stalin 'doctored' the photograph and removed Trotsky and Kamenev. They were both leaders of the Russian revolution and linked to Lenin. They were rivals of Stalin in the struggle for leadership of the Soviet Union after Lenin's death in 1924. Stalin wanted total power which involved 'removing' both Trotsky and Kamenev and any memory of them. He therefore had both of them killed and attempted to remove them from history. They were taken out of the photograph of Lenin and the doctored picture then appeared in school history textbooks used throughout the Soviet Union.

Question 2 As the pictures in Item A show, historical evidence is sometimes changed for political reasons. In this case, the picture of Lenin was faked to reinforce Stalin's rule.

Historical evidence can be 'doctored' or forged for a variety of reasons. In the case of Hitler's diaries, money appears to be a major reason for forgery – *Stern* magazine paid $4 million for the fake diaries.

It is important for historians to question the credibility of historical evidence. If Hitler's diaries had been accepted as the genuine article, then history would have been, to some extent, re-written. As it was, the fake diaries led to the discovery that letters, supposedly written by Hitler, were also forgeries.

Activity 2 Peasants in Medieval England (p53)

Peasants were at the bottom of the social hierarchy in Medieval England. They could not read or write and so they left no written records about their way of life. As a result, their voices are unheard. Historians must reconstruct their way of life from evidence left by the literate and powerful. A few pictures from illustrated manuscripts, usually written by monks, give us a glimpse of peasant life. Apart from this, the main evidence is provided by legal documents which state their obligations to the lord of the manor and detail the punishments they received for failing to meet these obligations. Neither the pictorial nor the written evidence gives the peasants' point of view.

Historians need to use their imagination in order to reconstruct the peasants' way of life from the relatively few pieces of information available. Because of the scarcity of documentary evidence and the fact that it reflects the perspectives of the powerful, the credibility of historians' accounts of peasant life should be questioned.

Activity 3 Problems of evidence (p55)

Item A shows that what people say they will do and what they actually do can be two different things. The young Chinese-American couple were only once refused service in the 250 hotels, restaurants and campsites they visited. Yet, in reply to a letter sent by the researcher, 92% of these establishments said quite categorically that they would refuse service to Chinese Americans. This research suggests that we should query people's responses to questions which ask them what they would do in particular situations.

Item B indicates that when people say they have seen or done something, we should not necessarily believe them. In this case, 40% of the children claimed to have seen at least one of the fictional films on the list. This does not necessarily mean that they are consciously lying. Memory plays strange tricks – many of the children might well believe they have actually seen one or more of the films.

Questions in interviews and questionnaires often ask people what they have seen, done or will do. In view of the evidence in Items A and B, we should be wary of accepting their answers at face value.

Activity 4 *Incredible claims on the Internet (p57)*

Item A There have been many reports about meetings with aliens from outer space. Most people are aware of stories about such meetings by reading about them in newspapers and magazines and from watching movies. However, there is a lack of independent corroborative evidence to support these stories. In other words, we must rely on the claims of those who supposedly met the aliens. Without independent corroborative evidence, the credibility of such claims is low.

In the case outlined in Item A, there is some evidence to support the claims of the four men. All told the same story when hypnotised and all took a lie detector test which indicated that they were telling the truth. However, all this suggests is that the men actually believed that they had an encounter with aliens. Again, we have to rely on the men's claims.

Why did the four men tell this story? First, there is a very slight possibility that the event occurred. Second, assuming they did not meet aliens, something may have occurred – for example, the round, glowing object. Third, let's assume that the nightmares had no connection with what happened. However, as the men discussed the nightmares and the 'strange event', the two may have become connected. Fourth, this may have become a 'false memory'. Psychologists have shown how it is possible to implant false memories of events which never happened, to the point where people actually believe that those events happened. Following this line of argument, the meeting with the aliens in all probability did not occur. As a result, the story told by the four men has little or no credibility.

Item B Hundreds, if not thousands, of weeping icons and statues have been reported over the last thousand or so years. There is little doubt that some kind of liquid emerged from the general area of the eyes in these cases. The question is, did a miracle occur? Clearly, some people believe in miracles. In the examples given in Item B, many believed that 'weeping' did occur and saw it as evidence of a miracle. However, apart from their religious beliefs, there is no way of proving that a miracle occurred.

There are, however, plenty of ways of providing non-religious, scientific explanations to account for the 'weeping'. In the case of weeping icons, resin from the oil used in the paint can, under certain conditions, become moist and run. When this occurs in areas other than the eyes, it will probably be seen as inconsequential. However, if it appears to be coming from the eyes, then certain people with strong religious beliefs may see it as a miracle. In the case of Mrs Murray's weeping Madonna, the manufacturers provide an explanation – the adhesive used to attach the eyes can become moist at certain temperatures and this may account for the 'tears'.

The argument presented above suggests that there is little support for the claims that weeping icons and statues should be seen as miracles.

Unit 12   Making a reasoned judgement

Activity 1 *Making a reasoned judgement (p62)*

Corroborative evidence

This refers to pieces of evidence which support each other, which agree and point in the same direction. There are four sources which suggest that violent films lead to violent behaviour.

⚙ **Newspaper reports** They make the general claim that violent films lead to violent behaviour. And they make the specific claim that there are significant similarities between scenes in *Child's Play 3* and the killing of James Bulger. The suggestion is that the boys who killed James Bulger had been influenced by the video and acted out what they had seen.

⚙ **The trial judge** During the boys' trial, the judge mentioned that the stepfather of one of the boys had a collection of violent videos. The judge stated, 'I suspect that exposure to violent films may in part be an explanation'.

⚙ **Reaction in Parliament** The reaction of the MPs quoted supports the view that violent films lead to violent behaviour. For example, Sir Ivan Lawrence claims that the 'constant diet of violence' in the media produces violent behaviour in young people.

⚙ **Expert judgement** This view is supported by some academic research. Professor Newson's report concludes that there is a strong link between violent films and real-life violence and that violent films can lead to violent behaviour.

Conflicting evidence

This refers to pieces of evidence which do not support each other, which do not agree and which point in different directions.

⚙ **Merseyside police detectives** They found no evidence that the two boys had watched *Child's Play 3*. Nor did they find any evidence from the videos rented by the boys' parents that might have encouraged them to do what they did. This conflicts with the evidence outlined above.

⚙ **Expert judgement** Researchers at the University of Birmingham reject Professor Newson's view. They argue that violence in the home leads to violent behaviour which, in turn, is likely to lead to a preference for violent films.

Balance of evidence

The balance of evidence outlines and explains which sources support each side of the dispute. It involves identifying the sources which 1) support the conclusion that violent films are *more likely* to lead to violent behaviour and 2) identifying sources which support the conclusion that violent films are *less likely* to lead to violent behaviour.

More likely The tabloid newspapers, particularly the *Sun* and the *Mail*, all claim that violent films lead to violent behaviour and that *Child's Play 3* directly influenced the killing of James Bulger. The trial judge 'suspected' that exposure to violent films may in part explain the boys' behaviour. The reaction of MPs supports the general claim that violent films cause violent behaviour, as does Professor Newson's report.

Less likely The police investigation found no evidence that the two boys had watched *Child's Play 3*. Nor did it reveal any evidence that the videos rented by the boys' parents contained scenes which might have influenced the boys' behaviour. The Birmingham University study argues that a violent home background rather than violent films leads to violent behaviour. The social and family background of the two boys supports this view.

Weight of evidence

This refers to the number of sources of evidence which support the 'more likely' conclusion and the number which support the 'less likely' conclusion. It involves adding up the sources in the balance of evidence, as shown below.

More likely	Less likely
Reports in tabloid newspapers	Police investigation
The trial judge's view	Birmingham University research
Reaction in Parliament	Family background of boys
Professor Newson's report	
Total 4	**Total 3**

The weight of evidence (4:3) suggests that it is more likely that violent films lead to violent behaviour. However, 4:3 is fairly close, so the weight of evidence does not provide strong support for this conclusion. And it is important to remember that the weight of evidence says nothing about the quality of evidence.

Quality of evidence

The quality of evidence refers to the credibility of the sources and the evidence they provide. Are the sources believable? Is the evidence they provide reliable? It is very important to assess credibility. For example, if the four sources in the 'more likely' column lack credibility then they will *not* support the conclusion that violent films lead to violent behaviour. Here is a brief assessment of the credibility of the sources.

1 The tabloids In general, the tabloid press does not have a particularly good reputation for reliability. It tends to sensationalise and often fails to provide 'hard' evidence to support its claims. The tabloids report the common-sense view that violent films lead to violent behaviour, but provide little or no evidence to support this claim. In addition, they claim that scenes from *Child's Play 3* have significant similarities to the murder of James Bulger. Again, they fail to back up this claim with detailed evidence.

2 The trial judge Judges are experts on the law, not on the effects of the media on the behaviour of young people. Because of this, his claim that 'exposure to violent films may in part be an explanation' has little credibility.

3 Reaction in Parliament The quotes from the two MPs contain claims but no evidence to support those claims. For example, Ivan Lawrence simply states that it is becoming 'daily more obvious' that 'the constant diet of violence and depravity' in the media leads to increasingly violent behaviour in young people. All he is doing here is re-stating the common-sense view that violent films lead to violent behaviour. As such, this is simply one person's opinion which lacks any supporting evidence.

4 Professor Newson's report As an academic, Elizabeth Newson has a high reputation. She also has relevant expertise in child psychology. Her report is based on a survey of newspaper reports and academic studies. It concludes that there is a strong link between violent films and real-life violence. Because of her reputation and expertise, Professor Newson's report has high credibility.

5 The police investigation Although they are not experts in the relationship between media output and behaviour, the police detectives have been trained to investigate crimes. Judging from reports in the *Independent*, a newspaper with a reputation for reliability, the police investigation was extremely thorough. There was no evidence that the boys had seen *Child's Play 3*. And there was nothing in the 200 videos rented by the boys' parents 'where you could put your finger on the freeze button and say that influenced a boy to go out and commit murder'.

6 University of Birmingham research As academics with relevant expertise, the team of psychologists at Birmingham University are a credible source. They argue that a violent home background can lead to violent behaviour which, in turn, is likely to lead to a preference for violent films.

7 Social and family background Evidence indicates that the boys came from violent families and had a history of violent behaviour. Part of the evidence comes from NSPCC conference notes written by social workers who had dealt with the boys and their parents. The NSPCC is a reputable charity. Part of the evidence comes from the *Guardian* online, a highly reputable source and from wikipedia.org, an online encyclopaedia with a good reputation for reliability.

Conclusion

The first four sources support the view that violent films are likely to lead to violent behaviour. However, most of these sources are based on little more than opinion and common sense. The tabloids had been conducting a campaign against 'video nasties' before the murder occurred. James Bulger's killing was seen as a justification for this campaign. However, the tabloids presented little or no hard evidence to support their claims. This criticism also applies to the trial judge and to the MPs. In fact, the police were taken aback when they heard the judge state that violent films had probably influenced the boys' behaviour. After their lengthy investigation, one detective said, 'I don't know where the judge got that idea from. I couldn't believe it when I heard him.'

Unlike the above sources, Professor Newson's report is a credible source. It is based on a survey of academic research and newspaper reports and concludes that there is a strong link between violent films and violent behaviour.

Overall, as noted earlier, the three sources which indicate that violent films are unlikely to lead to violent behaviour have greater credibility. First, the police investigation is a thorough examination of the possible link between violent videos and the James Bulger murder. It concludes: 'If you are going to link this murder to a film, you might as well link it to the *Railway Children*'. Second, the Birmingham University research provides an explanation for the apparent causal link between violent films and violent behaviour. It states that a violent home background can lead to violent behaviour which, in turn, is likely to lead to a preference for violent films. This view is supported by the evidence on the violent home background of the two boys. And, if they did watch the violent films which their parents rented, the Birmingham research suggests why they might enjoy these films. But the research states clearly that it is not the films which are the cause of the boys' behaviour. Instead, it is their violent home background which causes both violent behaviour and a liking for violent films.

The above conclusion leads to a reasoned judgement that violent films are unlikely to lead to violent behaviour.

Unit 13 What is an argument?

Activity 1 *Arguments and non-arguments (p64)*

Question 1 *a)* The answer is C. An argument must consist of at least one reason and a conclusion. Statement A is not an argument because there is no reason to support the claim that weather forecasts are usually reliable. Similarly, statement B does not have a reason to support the claim that weather forecasts are sometimes unreliable. Although statement D has two sentences, there is still no argument. The two claims merely state the same thing in slightly different ways. C is the answer because there is a reason and a conclusion. The conclusion is that 'weather forecasts may be unreliable' and the reason is that 'it is difficult to forecast weather patterns accurately'.

b) The answer is B. Statements A and D are both claims which are not supported by reasons. Statement C is not an argument, it is merely an expression of dislike. B is the answer because there is a reason and a conclusion. The conclusion is that 'some Indian food may be hot' and the reason is that 'it contains chilli'.

Question 2 *a)* In this argument the conclusion is stated in the first sentence. It is that 'The traffic congestion charge levied on vehicles in the centre of London has been a great success'. The reason is stated in the second sentence and is because 'Delays are down by 30%'.

b) The conclusion in this argument is that the £600,000 spent improving the park was a waste of money. The reason is because the money could have been better spent employing more teachers in the primary school where they are short-staffed.

Activity 2 *The structure of simple arguments (p65)*

Question 1 *a)* An argument indicator is a word or phrase which links a reason to a conclusion in an argument. Indicators are normally used when a reason and a conclusion are expressed in the same sentence. In this case the argument indicator is the word 'because'. It links the conclusion in the argument, 'Rottnest is safe for cyclists' to the reason which is 'cars are not allowed on the island'.

b) In this argument, the argument indicator is the word 'therefore'. It links the reason 'Several people have died in Turkey after contracting bird flu' to the conclusion which is 'it may not be safe to go there for a holiday'.

Question 2 When rewriting this argument with the reason in the first sentence, it will be necessary to use an argument indicator in the second sentence. The rewritten argument is shown below and the argument indicator is 'therefore'. The indicators 'so' or 'as a result' might also be used.

Internet shopping is so convenient and goods are usually cheaper than they are in the shops. Therefore, Internet shopping is becoming increasingly popular.

Activity 3 *Unit review (p66)*

Question 1 a) The conclusion in this argument is the first sentence 'Channel 4's *Big Brother* is trash'. It is supported by the second sentence which contains some reasons.

b) The argument can be rewritten as follows using the argument indicator 'because'.

Channel 4's Big Brother is trash because it is boring, shallow and childish.

c) Symbolically the argument can be presented as follows.

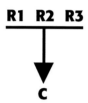

R1, R2 and R3 represent the three reasons – that *Big Brother* is boring, shallow and childish – to support the conclusion, C, that the programme is trash.

Question 2 a) The reason in this argument is the first sentence 'Evidence suggests that university students are some of the poorest young people in society'. This is used to support the conclusion that students should not have to pay towards their education.

b) Symbolically the argument can be presented as follows.

This argument has only one reason R and a conclusion C. The arrow shows the direction of reasoning – that the reason leads to the conclusion.

c) A number of other reasons could be used to support the conclusion in this argument. Some examples are given below.

✪ Students do not have time to earn money while studying full-time.

✪ Some students come from poor family backgrounds and their parents cannot provide them with financial support.

✪ The number of university applications has fallen since the introduction of tuition fees.

✪ Society as a whole benefits from higher education, so society should pay via the tax system.

Question 3 a) The answer is B. The conclusion is found in the first sentence, ie that 'the world economy is set to grow'. The sentences that follow are the reasons given to support the conclusion. Statement A is not the conclusion in the argument. It is a reason that supports the conclusion, ie that economic forecasters believe that global growth will be 4.5% in 2006. Statement D is also a reason that supports the conclusion, ie that stock markets around the world are buoyant. Statement C may be a conclusion but not the one in this argument. In this statement, the growth of the world economy is said to be dependent on the performance of the Japanese economy. This is not part of the argument shown here.

b) There are three reasons to support the conclusion in this argument. Symbolically it can be presented as follows:

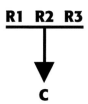

Unit 14 Identifying reasons in arguments

Activity 1 *Reason indicators (p67)*

Question 1 *a)* Reasons are used in arguments to support a conclusion. In this argument, the conclusion is that smokers should quit smoking if they want to live longer. The reason for this is that 'smoking causes life-threatening diseases'.

b) Reason indicators are words or phrases which indicate that a reason is being given to support a conclusion in an argument. In this argument, the reason is expressed at the beginning of the sentence. The very first word 'since' is the reason indicator.

Question 2 *a)* In this argument the reason is given in the second half of the sentence. The conclusion is that 'Gerry could not have stolen the cash from the till'. The reason is that 'he was in the storeroom discussing new product lines with the manager'.

b) The reason indicator is to be found in the middle of the sentence. It is the word 'because' and it links the reason to the conclusion.

Activity 2 *Adding reason indicators (p68)*

Question 1 *a)* The reason in this argument is contained in the first sentence. It is 'Double glazing helps to keep heat inside a building'. This reason is used to support the conclusion that 'fitting double glazing is likely to reduce fuel bills'.

b) The argument can be rewritten using a reason indicator. It is shown below with the reason indicator written in bold.

*Fitting double glazing is likely to reduce fuel bills **because** double glazing helps to keep heat inside a building.*

Other reason indicators might be used, for example, 'since'.

Question 2 *a)* In this argument, the conclusion is that 'there should be a tax on flying'. This is stated in the first sentence. The two reasons to support this conclusion are given in the second sentence. They are:

✪ pollution from jets is damaging the environment;

✪ global oil supplies are diminishing rapidly.

b) The argument can be rewritten using a reason indicator. It is shown below with the reason indicator written in bold.

There should be a tax on flying **because** *pollution from jets damages the environment and global oil supplies are diminishing rapidly.*

Again, other indicators could have been used such as 'since' or 'firstly…secondly'.

Activity 3 *Using evidence to support reasons (p69)*

Question 1 *a)* The conclusion in this argument is written in the first sentence. It is 'Bird flu moved closer to Britain in February 2006'.

b) The reason in this argument is stated in the second sentence. It is due to the westward migration of infected birds.

c) Evidence provides support for reasons and can help make an argument stronger. In this argument, the evidence to support the claim that birds infected with bird flu migrated westwards is contained in the last two sentences. Cases of bird flu were identified in Turkey as birds travelled west from Asia. And then in Greece, Italy and France, as birds continued their westward migration. If this evidence is credible, it provides support for the reason.

Question 2 *a)* The conclusion in this argument is given in the first sentence. It is that 'Wine drinkers have fewer illnesses than beer drinkers'.

b) The reason for the conclusion is contained at the end of the first sentence. It is that wine drinkers buy healthier food than beer drinkers.

c) The argument contains evidence to support this reason. The evidence is outlined in the next two sentences. It comes from a study carried out by Danish researchers. The study showed that typical wine drinkers bought more olives, fruit and vegetables, poultry, low-fat cheese and skimmed milk. On the other hand, beer drinkers tended to buy less healthy food such as ready-meals, chips, butter, sausages and soft drinks.

Activity 4 Unit review *(p70)*

Question 1 *a)* Writing arguments in standard form helps to separate the reasons from the conclusion and the evidence. This argument is presented in standard form below.

R1 Bonding with friends has beneficial mental and physical effects.
R2 Socialising boosts the immune system.

C Spending time with your friends is good for your health.

b) The argument is presented symbolically below.

R1   R2

C

c) One piece of evidence in the argument is provided by American researchers. The evidence supports the second reason that socialising boosts the immune system. The researchers report that socialising boosts the immune system by increasing the amount of immunoglobins and T-cells in the body, which, in turn, fight infections and tumours. If the research evidence is credible, this provides strong support for the reason and hence the argument.

Question 2 *a)* The argument presented in standard form is shown below.

R1 Yoga helps to prevent and alleviate a number of ailments.
R2 Yoga can help to burn fat and reduce weight.
R3 Yoga can help to develop and tone muscle.
_____

C Yoga is a good way of improving one's mind, body and spirit.

b) The argument is presented symbolically below.

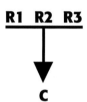

c) The argument contains quite a lot of evidence to support the reasons. For example, the ailments that yoga is said to prevent or alleviate include back and shoulder pain, asthma, headaches and stress.

There is also some evidence which supports the claim that yoga burns fat and reduces weight. For example, deep breathing increases oxygen intake which helps the body to burn fat.

There is also evidence which supports the claim that yoga can develop muscle. For example, certain postures stimulate glands, such as the thyroid, in their secretion of hormones, and increase the metabolism so that fat is converted into muscle.

Unit 15 Identifying conclusions in arguments

Activity 1 *Conclusion indicators (p71)*

Question 1 *a)* Conclusions in arguments are very important. The purpose of an argument is to persuade others to accept the conclusion. The conclusion in this argument is that Elaine is a prime suspect for the theft of money from the office safe.

Conclusion indicators can be used to help identify conclusions in arguments. They are words or phrases that indicate that a conclusion is being given in an argument. In this argument, the conclusion indicator is 'must' in the phrase 'she must be a prime suspect'.

b) The conclusion in this argument is that the Queen's Head is a rough pub. The conclusion indicator is the phrase 'indicates that' in the sentence 'This indicates that it is a rough pub'.

c) In this argument, the conclusion is that urgent steps must be taken to deal with the problems of truancy, poor exam results and discipline in a local secondary school. A conclusion indicator in this argument is the phrase 'shows that' in the sentence 'This shows that urgent steps must be taken to put matters right'. The word 'must' is an additional conclusion indicator.

Question 2 *a)* The answer is B. A is not the answer. First, the reference in the argument to male attention is a reason given for cosmetic breast surgery. In addition, there is no mention of male attention 'justifying' breast surgery. C is evidence which is used as a reason to support the conclusion. D is irrelevant to the argument and is not stated in the passage. B is the conclusion – it is drawn from the two reasons given in the argument, the increase in cosmetic breast surgery and the increase in anti-aging surgery.

b) The conclusion indicator in this argument is the phrase 'demonstrate that', as used in the last sentence.

Activity 2 *Conclusions without indicators (p73)*

Question 1 The conclusion indicators, which have been added to the argument, are shown in bold.

a) Tipping waste material harms the environment, **hence***, recycling household rubbish can help this problem.*

b) There is a shortage of leisure facilities in many inner cities, **consequently***, children in these areas often have to play in the street.*

c) People living in poverty have a shorter life expectancy and suffer more illness, **therefore***, poverty is a social evil.*

Note Other conclusion indicators might also be used in these arguments.

Question 2 *a)* The answer is C because it draws together the two main claims made in the argument – that tax relief on research and development expenditure by businesses would increase the benefits to society. Statement A is about the possible link between business competitiveness and tax relief – it says nothing about the benefits of research and development to society. B links research and development with benefits to society but does not mention tax relief. D states that the government should help businesses by raising tax relief on research and development expenditure but says nothing about benefits to society.

b) The last two sentences in the argument are rewritten below with a conclusion indicator. The conclusion indicator is shown in bold.

As a result *of the government raising tax relief on research and development expenditure, business would spend more and the benefits to society would increase.*

Activity 3 *Unit review (p74)*

Question 1 *a)* The conclusion in this argument is that 'Bangladesh is the worst team in test match cricket'.

b) This argument is rewritten below with a conclusion indicator.

Bangladesh have only ever won a single test match, **therefore***, they are the worst team in test cricket.*

Question 2 *a)* The main conclusion in this argument is that 'Montgomery is warm-blooded'.

b) The answer is B. Statement A is a reason in the argument. Statement C is the main conclusion in the argument. Statement D is another reason in the argument. The answer is B because the claim 'Montgomery is a mammal' follows on from two other claims that are given as reasons, ie 'Montgomery is a cat' and 'All cats are mammals'. This is an intermediate conclusion and not the main conclusion because the argument continues.

c) There are two conclusion indicators in this argument. The first is used to indicate the intermediate conclusion in the second sentence. It is the word 'so'. The second is used to indicate the main conclusion in the argument in the final sentence. It is the phrase 'it follows that'.

Question 3 *a)* The main conclusion in this argument is that plans to build another toll road on the M6 are misguided. This is stated in the final sentence and follows from the reasons and the intermediate conclusion.

b) The intermediate conclusion in this argument is that building the M6 toll road was a waste of resources. This follows from the two reasons that much of the time it is nearly empty and it was also expensive to build.

c) There are two conclusion indicators in this argument. The first is used to indicate the intermediate conclusion which follows from the two reasons. It is the word 'therefore' in the sentence 'It was very expensive to build and therefore a waste of resources'. The second is used to indicate the main conclusion and is the word 'consequently'. The indicator is the first word in the final sentence.

Unit 16 Patterns of reasoning

Activity 1 *Side-by-side reasoning (p76)*

Question 1 *a)* The conclusion in this argument is that 'Profits are bound to fall in the next financial year'. Three reasons are given to support this claim.

✪ Competition is intensifying which means the company will lose market share.

✪ Rising fuel prices will raise the company's costs.

✪ Overseas sales will fall due to rising exchange rates.

b) Side-by-side reasoning involves using more than one reason to support the same conclusion. However, the reasons are independent of each other. This means that any one of the reasons can be used on its own to support the conclusion. In this argument, any one of the three reasons given can support the same conclusion. For example, the first reason 'Competition is intensifying which means we will probably lose market share', is sufficient to support the conclusion 'profits are bound to fall in the next financial year'.

Question 2 *a)* This argument presented in standard form is shown below.

R1 A number of accidents have resulted in shoppers being injured.
R2 Traffic fumes can make shopping on Market Street unpleasant.
R3 Providing seats for people to relax will make shopping less stressful.

C Market Street should be pedestrianised.

b) This argument uses side-by-side reasoning. Each of the three reasons can be used independently. This means that any one of the reasons can be used on its own to support the conclusion. For example, in this argument, the first reason 'A number of accidents have resulted in shoppers being injured', is sufficient on its own to support the conclusion 'Market Street should be pedestrianised'.

Activity 2 *Joint reasoning (p77)*

Question 1 *a)* The argument is presented in standard form below.

R1 Women drivers have fewer accidents than men.
R2 Both female and male drivers aged over 25 have fewer accidents than drivers under 25.

_____

C Some insurance companies give lower rates of car insurance to women and all insurance companies give lower rates to drivers aged 25 and over.

b) The argument is presented symbolically below.

Note The positive (plus) sign between R1 and R2 shows that the reasons are acting jointly.

c) When using joint reasoning, the reasons in an argument have to be presented together. This means that a conclusion cannot be drawn unless all the reasons in the argument are used together. One of the reasons alone will not be sufficient to draw the conclusion. In this argument, the conclusion is that 'Some insurance companies give lower rates of car insurance to women and all insurance companies give lower rates to drivers aged 25 and over'. This conclusion could not be drawn, if for example, the first reason alone was used. This is because the first reason only relates to part of the conclusion (ie the part about cheaper premiums for women). Both of the reasons are needed to support the conclusion.

Question 2 *a)* The argument is presented in standard form below.

R1 The opposition will win by-elections if they become more popular.
R2 The opposition have not won any by-elections recently.

_____

C The opposition are unlikely to be gaining in popularity.

b) The argument is presented symbolically below.

c) Again, in this argument, joint reasoning is used. This is shown in the diagram in b) where a positive sign is placed between the two reasons. In this argument the conclusion, 'the opposition are unlikely to be gaining in popularity', cannot be supported by one of the reasons alone. For example, if we take the first reason 'the opposition will win by-elections if they become more popular', this claim is not sufficient to support the conclusion. This is because we do not know whether the opposition has won or lost any recent by-elections. We need to know this to draw the conclusion.

Activity 3 *Unit review (pp78-79)*

Question 1 *a)* The argument is presented in standard form below.

R1 Glaciers are melting.
R2 The polar ice caps are shrinking.
R3 Sea levels are rising.
R4 Deserts are expanding.

_____

C Global warming is occurring.

b) The argument is presented symbolically below.

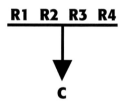

c) In this argument, the pattern of reasoning used is side-by-side. All of the reasons presented act independently. The conclusion can be supported if any one of the reasons given is used alone. For example, the second reason 'The polar ice caps are shrinking' provides a good enough reason to draw the conclusion 'global warming is occurring'.

Question 2 *a)* The argument is presented in standard form below.

R1 More people of working age are needed to support Britain's aging population.
R2 The present level of immigration can supply some of these people, but not enough.
IC Further measures are therefore needed.
R3 An increase in the birth rate will lead to more people of working age.

C The government should encourage couples to have more children.

b) The argument is presented symbolically below.

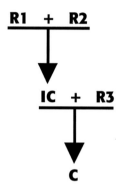

c) The first two reasons in this argument are joint reasons as shown in the diagram in b). Both reasons are needed to draw the intermediate conclusion that further measures are needed to increase the number of working people. One of these reasons alone would not be sufficient. For example, the first reason 'More people of working age are needed to support Britain's aging population' does not allow us to draw the conclusion because we do not know that the number of immigrants is going to be inadequate. The second reason tells us this. Therefore the first reason alone is not sufficient to draw the intermediate conclusion.

Question 3 *a)* The argument is presented in standard form below.

R1 Breast feeding provides babies with a highly nutritious diet.
IC1 Therefore breast feeding should be encouraged.
R2 If babies are hungry and not fed they become distressed.
IC2 Therefore mothers should be able to breast feed wherever they are.
R3 Sometimes mothers may not be able to find somewhere private to breast feed.

C Mothers should be able to breast feed in public.

b) The argument is presented symbolically below.

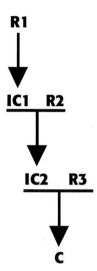

c) This argument uses chain reasoning. This means that a number of reasons and intermediate conclusions are used in sequence to draw a main conclusion. The structure resembles a chain. In this argument, the first intermediate conclusion 'breast feeding should be encouraged' is drawn from the first reason 'breast feeding provides babies with a highly nutritious diet'.

The second intermediate conclusion 'mothers should be able to breast feed wherever they are' is drawn from the first intermediate conclusion (which becomes a reason) and the second reason 'If babies are hungry and not fed they become distressed'.

The main conclusion that 'mothers should be able to breast feed in public' is drawn from the second intermediate conclusion (which becomes another reason) and a third reason 'Sometimes mothers may not be able to find somewhere private to breast feed'.

Unit 17 Deductive and inductive arguments

Activity 1 *Deductive arguments (p80)*

Question 1 The answer is B. Both arguments are deductive.

In both cases the conclusion is guaranteed to follow from the reasons. This can be seen from Argument 1. If all dogs are mammals, and a poodle is a dog, then a poodle must be a mammal. Logically, the conclusion must follow from the reasons. As a result, this is a deductive argument. In this case, both reasons are true, therefore the conclusion must also be true.

The same applies to Argument 2. Logically, the conclusion must follow from the reasons – it is guaranteed to do so. The argument is therefore deductive. As with Argument 1, both reasons are true, therefore the conclusion must also be true.

Question 2 The answer is A. Argument 1 is deductive and Argument 2 is not.

Argument 1 In Argument 1, the logic of the argument cannot be faulted. The conclusion necessarily follows from the reasons. The argument states that all birds can fly and an ostrich is a bird. Given this, it logically follows that an ostrich can fly. Since the conclusion is guaranteed to follow from the reasons, the argument is therefore deductive.

In this case, the first reason is not true, because not all birds can fly. As a result, the conclusion is not true, since ostriches cannot fly.

When classifying an argument as deductive, we are not concerned with the truth or the accuracy of the reasons. Instead, we are concerned with the logic of the argument. Argument 1 is a deductive argument simply because the conclusion is logically guaranteed to follow from the reasons.

Note Students often have trouble with a deductive argument which is not true. This type of deductive argument is examined in Unit 24, page 109.

Argument 2 This is not a deductive argument because the conclusion does not necessarily follow from the reasons. Just because Jackie has a brain does not necessarily mean she is a human being. She might be any living creature with a brain – a dog, an elephant, a dolphin, or somebody's pet hamster. Jackie may be a human being, but the reasons given in the argument do not guarantee that she is human. Because of this lack of certainty, Argument 2 is not a deductive argument.

Activity 2 *Inductive arguments* (p81)

Question 1 *a)* The conclusion in this argument is that the garlic chicken, eaten by Jennifer and two of her five friends at the Belle View restaurant, was the cause of their illness.

b) In an inductive argument, if the reasons are true, then the conclusion will probably be true. But only probably – the certainty of deductive arguments is lacking. In this argument, it is likely that the garlic chicken caused the illness because the three people who became ill all ate the garlic chicken. However, this conclusion cannot be drawn with certainty. It is possible that something else caused the illness. The three people may have all eaten something else that the others had not consumed. It is also possible that something consumed by all of the people was 'off' but only three people were actually ill. Alternatively, it may not have been the food at all – a virus perhaps, picked up by one and passed on to two others.

Question 2 The conclusion in this argument is that Shell should have to pay a windfall tax on its 2005 profits. Two reasons are given in the argument. The first is that Shell made a record £12.93bn profit in 2005. The second is that the profit was due mainly to the rapid rise in oil prices during the year. This is an inductive argument because the conclusion is only probably true. Many people would accept the conclusion because the huge profits made by Shell were not necessarily the result of good business management. They were helped along considerably by the very high oil price in 2005. Many people would also agree that a profit of £12.93 bn is excessive. However, some would not accept the conclusion, Shell shareholders for example, and therefore the conclusion is not certain and the argument is inductive not deductive.

Activity 3 *Unit review (p83)*

Question 1 *a)* The conclusion in this argument is that ears of corn always have an even number of rows. It is an inductive argument.

b) This argument is inductive because the conclusion cannot be drawn from the reasons given with any certainty. The author of the argument has been eating corn on the cob for years and always counts the number of rows. The author has never found an ear of corn with an odd number of rows. However, other people who eat corn on the cob may have found an ear of corn with an odd number of rows. We cannot be absolutely sure that the conclusion is true, therefore the argument is inductive.

Question 2 *a)* The answer is D. Argument 1 is inductive and Argument 2 is deductive.

Argument 1 The conclusion in this argument is that the workforce is sure to accept the 2.6% pay deal offered by management. The reasons given to support this claim are that workers will be provided with subsidised meals when the new canteen is built and that a more substantial offer is promised after the new working practices have been introduced. This conclusion cannot be drawn with certainty. The workers may decide to reject the offer. Therefore the argument is inductive.

Argument 2 The conclusion in this argument is that oxygen is not molecular. This conclusion is guaranteed to follow from the reasons. If oxygen is an element, and no elements are molecular, then oxygen cannot be molecular. Logically, the conclusion must follow from the reasons. As a result, this is a deductive argument. In this case, both reasons are true, therefore the conclusion must also be true.

Question 3 *a)* The argument is presented in standard form below.

R1 Gaining qualifications can open up new career opportunities.
R2 Gaining qualifications can provide a route into university.
R3 Night school provides an opportunity to meet people and make new friends.
R4 Night school helps people to reach their full potential.

C Attending night school can be extremely beneficial to adults.

b) This argument contains quite a lot of evidence. For example, the first reason is supported by the fact that around a quarter of adult students either changed jobs or gained promotion in their existing jobs. The second reason is supported by the fact that, over the last few years, around one fifth of adult students went on to university. The fourth reason is supported by evidence from course evaluation questionnaires which reported that over half of adult students said that they had achieved qualifications that they previously thought were beyond them.

c) Many arguments contain background information. Background information should be ignored when analysing and evaluating arguments. Examples of background information in this argument include the following.

✪ West Righton FE College is bordered by woodland and meadows.

✪ The college offers evening courses in subjects such as AS and A Level Business Studies, Economics, Sociology, Critical Thinking, Media Studies, Maths, French and English.

✪ The cost of enrolling for an AS course at West Righton is £100 and £175 for an A Level course.

Unit 18 Assumptions in arguments

Activity 1 *Assumptions (p84)*

Question 1 *a)* Many arguments contain assumptions. Usually, they are so obvious that they are not worth spelling out. This argument provides a good example. The argument assumes that children should not be exposed to explicit content, such as the glamorisation of violence, the treatment of women as sex objects and swearing, without parental consent. This assumption is necessary to accept the conclusion that 'Rap CDs should carry parental advisory labels'.

b) The argument is presented in standard form below. The assumption has been added as another reason.

R1 Rap music often glamorises violence.
R2 Rap music often treats women as sex objects.
R3 Rap music often contains swearing.
R4 Children should not be exposed to explicit content without parental consent.

C Rap CDs should carry parental advisory labels.

Question 2 *a)* In this argument the conclusion is that the levels of saturated fat in crisps should be reduced. The assumption is that high levels of saturated fat are undesirable or even harmful. This is not stated but must be assumed for the conclusion to be accepted.

b) Making assumptions does not necessarily weaken arguments. In arguments like this one, there is no need to state all the reasons to draw the conclusion. It is obvious to most people that high levels of saturated fat are undesirable. Making assumptions can help to present an argument more concisely and give it greater impact.

Question 3 *a)* In this argument the conclusion is that 'the price of drinks should be cut'. The assumption here is that a price cut will generate more sales of soft drinks.

b) The assumption in this argument is crucial if the conclusion is to be accepted. There is no point in reducing the price of soft drinks unless we believe that this will increase sales. This assumption is necessary to draw the conclusion.

Activity 2 *Unit review (p86)*

Question 1 In this argument the conclusion is that Jesus can perform miracles. However, the assumption is that walking on water and turning wine into water are miraculous achievements. This is not stated but must be assumed for the conclusion to be accepted.

Question 2 *a)* In this argument the conclusion is that 'whenever possible we should travel by train rather than fly'. The reason is because this will reduce global warming. The assumption here is that global warming is harmful.

b) It is possible to identify assumptions in arguments using the negative test. This involves changing the assumption to a negative statement. The argument is presented in standard form below with the assumption identified in a) written as a negative statement.

R1 Using trains instead of planes whenever possible will reduce greenhouse gases and global warming.

R2 Global warming is not harmful.

C We should travel by train instead of flying whenever possible.

The argument has now broken down. The negative form of the assumption contradicts the conclusion. It prevents the conclusion from being drawn. This means that the assumption has been identified correctly – global warming is harmful.

Question 3 *a)* The conclusion in this argument is that 'investors would be advised to invest in the stock market in 2006'.

b) The assumption in this argument is that the economic conditions that prevailed in 2005 will be likely to continue in 2006. For example, in 2005 the stock market rose by 15%, interest rates were only 5% and house prices rose by just 4.6%. If these conditions did prevail again in 2006, investing in the stock market would be very good advice. However, many would suggest that such an assumption is unrealistic. They would say that economic conditions are volatile and very uncertain in the future.

Question 4 The answer is C.

Statement A does not provide any support at all for the conclusion. It may also be untrue. The conclusion is that the government should insist that some test matches are screened on terrestrial television. This is to help maintain interest in the game. There is no evidence given in the argument to suggest that interest will return at the end of the SKY deal. This is not the assumption needed to draw the conclusion.

Although statement B may be true because it is in the interests of the ECB to generate interest in the game, it does not support the conclusion and is not the assumption upon which the conclusion is based. It has nothing to do with the government stepping in to insist that some test cricket is televised on free-to-air television.

Statement D may be true but is not the assumption required for the conclusion to be drawn. If interest in cricket does continue regardless of exposure on TV, this will not support the conclusion. The conclusion requires that cricket should benefit from TV exposure for it to thrive.

Statement C is the answer because interest in cricket will depend to a certain extent on the coverage it gets on television. This is the assumption that must be made if we believe that the government should step in and insist that some test cricket is televised on terrestrial television.

Unit 19 Principles in arguments

Activity 1 *Principles (p87)*

Question 1 C is the answer.

Most people believe that bribery, torture and selling personal information are wrong. These beliefs are principles. Statement C is not a principle. It is quite possible that more money is needed by the NHS to cope with the demands of an aging population, but it is not a medical ethic. It does not state the way something should be and is, therefore, not a principle.

Question 2 D is the answer.

Slavery is against human rights. Interfering with nature can be highly dangerous and is unethical. Purchasers accepting gifts from suppliers is unethical. Statement D 'Peaceful demonstrations are on the increase' is not a principle. It is just a piece of information. It does not state the way something should be.

Question 3 A is the answer.

B, C and D are all statements which may be true. For example, few would doubt that smoking-related illnesses cost the NHS millions of pounds. However, they are not principles. They do not state the way something should be. Statement A is a principle and is suggesting that self-inflicted illnesses should not be treated free of charge. The statement is saying the way something should be.

Activity 2 *Principles in arguments (p88)*

Question 1 *a)* B is the answer.

All of the statements A, B, C and D contain the word 'should' which suggests that they may all be principles. However, only B is a general principle. The other three statements are too specific to be general principles. For example, statement A says that footballers should pay more tax than office managers. Such a statement is too specific and does not have the characteristics of a moral guideline, a legal rule or a particular set of ethics. Statement B is a general principle with which many people would agree. The burden of tax should fall more heavily on those who can afford it. According to this principle, high earning footballers should pay more tax than office managers.

b) The conclusion in this argument is that there should be different rates of income tax which steadily rise from the rich, to the very rich to the super rich. This is the claim which is best described by statement B, the principle in the argument. This is that 'The burden of tax should fall more heavily on those who can afford it'. Therefore, in this argument, the principle is used as a conclusion.

Question 2 *a)* The principle in this argument is that self-inflicted illness should not be treated free of charge by the NHS. According to this principle, heavy drinkers who suffer from liver disease have only themselves to blame for their predicament. Therefore they should pay for their treatment because they know their behaviour is likely to harm their health.

b) In this argument the principle is used as a reason. The conclusion is that 'heavy drinkers who suffer from liver disease should pay for their medical treatment'. The reason is because their illness is self-inflicted and they know that their behaviour is likely to cause harm to their health. The general principle used here is that self-inflicted illness should not be treated free of charge by the NHS – it is used as a reason.

Activity 3 *Unit review (pp89-90)*

Question 1 D is the correct answer.

Statements A and C are too specific to be general principles. They focus on particular activities that involve the abuse of animals. For example, statement A is to do with the use of animals in experiments. Although many would agree with the statement, it is not a general principle. Statement B is just a fact. It is not a principle because it does not state the way something should be. D is the answer because it states that animals have rights and we should protect those rights – this is a general principle. It is a broad statement that states the way something should be.

Question 2 A is the correct answer.

Statements B, C and D are not general principles. Statement B is not the answer because it does not make any reference to the practice described in the passage. Individual business owners may charge what they like but in this argument business owners are colluding (getting together) to eliminate competition. They are not acting individually. Statement C is very similar to B. Individual business owners may charge what they like. However, they cannot collude in the way described in the argument. Statement D is not the answer because it is condoning the practice of price fixing. It is suggesting that consumers should accept the situation. Statement A is a general principle. It says that price fixing is wrong. The statement is stating the way that something ought to be.

Question 3 *a)* In this argument the conclusion is that 'capital punishment cannot be justified'.

b) The principle upon which the conclusion is based is stated in the last sentence in the argument. The principle is that killing people is wrong.

c) (i) Killing **might** be justified if:

- ✪ carried out in self-defence;
- ✪ carried out in a war situation;
- ✪ someone is terminally ill and suffering excruciating pain.

(ii) One of the problems of using principles in arguments is that they are inflexible – they cannot be bent to fit particular situations. They apply to every situation, to all circumstances. In this case, the principle is that killing people is wrong. If this is so, then killing people in self-defence, in a war situation or on compassionate grounds is also wrong. But many people would accept that killing people in these circumstances may be justified – this is the difficulty with using general principles.

(iii) To overcome the problem of inflexibility, principles may have to be modified. This means they have to be changed slightly to take into account the exceptions. For example, in this case, the principle might be rewritten as 'killing people is wrong except in self-defence, in a war situation and on compassionate grounds'.

Unit 20 Counter-arguments

Activity 1 Counter-arguments (p92)

Question 1 B is the correct answer.

A counter-argument is an argument which opposes another argument. Statement A is not a counter-argument. In fact, this statement is in agreement with the conclusion drawn in the argument – that cars contribute to global warming.

Statement C provides another possible reason for global warming by suggesting that volatile and unseasonal weather patterns are responsible. However, again, it does not provide the best counter-argument in this case because it does not make reference to exhaust fumes.

Statement D also provides another possible reason for global warming – cows! However, it provides no evidence to support its claim.

Statement B provides the best counter-argument. This is because it challenges directly the reason given in the argument and provides some statistical evidence to support its claim. It says that removing every vehicle from the world's highways would produce no discernible change to carbon dioxide levels in the atmosphere. The evidence provided is that 96.5% of all CO2 emissions are from natural sources, not man-made ones. This counters the original argument which states that one of the main contributors to global warming is emissions from vehicle exhausts.

Question 2 A is the correct answer.

Statement B does not challenge the argument, it supports it. This is because it agrees that the BMW driver is to blame for the accident by driving recklessly.

Statement C does not provide a convincing counter-argument. The statement provides another possible cause of the accident in that the Fiat driver's view of the main road was obscured by pedestrians. This may be true, but does not challenge directly the conclusion in the argument, ie that the collision was caused by the BMW driver.

Statement D suggests that car crashes are usually caused by a combination of factors. This may be true but is not a sound counter-argument in this case. It does not challenge directly the conclusion drawn in the argument.

A is the answer because it challenges directly the conclusion drawn in the argument. The statement places the blame squarely in the hands of the Fiat driver. This is because it says that the collision was caused by the Fiat driver. She should not have pulled out onto a main road until it was perfectly clear. This clears the BMW driver and provides the best counter-argument in this case.

Question 3 *a)* University students should not have to make a financial contribution to the cost of their education. Society in general benefits from people being educated to a higher level. Doctors, teachers, lawyers and other highly qualified people get the training they need to provide everyone with these specialist services.

b) This counter-argument challenges the reason given in the original argument. It explains how society as a whole benefits from a better educated population. It therefore implies that if everyone benefits, then everyone should pay, ie through the tax system.

Note It is also possible to produce a counter-argument using different reasons. For example, charging students might result in fewer university applications or discriminate against students from poorer family backgrounds.

Question 4 *a)* In this example, the counter-argument challenges the main reason given in the argument.

b) The argument says that dogs in the neighbourhood are a nuisance. They run wild and foul the pavement and people's gardens. This is the reason given for the conclusion that they should be 'put down'. The counter-argument challenges this reason by saying that it is not the dogs' fault, it is the responsibility of the owners who don't train them properly, who let them run lose and fail to clear up the mess. Consequently, if it is not the dogs' fault the conclusion cannot be accepted.

Activity 2 *Counter-arguments within arguments (p93)*

Question *a)* The main conclusion in this argument is that Wembley was the right location for the new national football stadium. A number of reasons are given to support this claim. For example, Wembley holds a special place in the hearts of football supporters all over the world. The conclusion in the counter-argument is that it was a mistake to build the national football stadium at Wembley. The reasons given in the counter-argument are that the cost of building the new stadium has escalated since the construction began and the stadium will not be completed for the 2006 FA Cup Final.

b) Using a counter-argument within an argument is a common method of presenting an argument. Counter-arguments are included in order to dismiss them. The counter-argument is presented as a target to be 'shot at'. In this case the counter-argument is that the cost of building the new stadium has escalated since the construction began and the stadium will not be completed for the 2006 FA Cup Final. However, it is also stated that 'although the cost is high, it is well worth it'. It also says that although the stadium will not be ready for the 2006 FA Cup Final, this is not really a problem because it will be used for all FA Cup Finals for another 100 years or more. Other reasons are added in the argument to strengthen it.

Activity 3 *Unit review (p94)*

Question 1 It is hypocritical, if not dishonest, for parents to allow their children to believe in something that they themselves know to be untrue. Therefore, belief in Santa Claus should be discouraged.

Note Other counter-arguments might include the following.

✪ Once children realise Santa doesn't exist, they will question everything else they were told to believe in, including God. If Santa turns out to be make-believe, maybe God is, too.

✪ By having children give Santa lists of presents they want, children learn to be materialistic.

✪ If the gifts they receive are attributed to Santa Claus, children will not be grateful to their parents for those gifts.

✪ Christian children should be taught to focus solely on the religious meaning of Christmas, and Santa Claus detracts from that.

Question 2 The counter-argument in this example suggests that there is a flaw in the reasoning produced in the original argument. The original argument claims that cannabis smokers are likely to become heroin addicts. This claim is based on another claim that many heroin addicts smoked cannabis before becoming heroin addicts. The reasoning is flawed because, as the counter-argument states, many heroin addicts drank orange juice before becoming heroin addicts but it is ludicrous to suggest that orange juice drinkers tend to become heroin addicts. The reasoning in the original argument is flawed because it is attempting to establish a cause and effect without any evidence. This is called a post hoc argument and is flawed.

Question 3 *a*) In this example, the counter-argument is challenging directly the main reason in the original argument.

***b*)** In the original argument it is claimed that fishing does not harm fish. The argument states 'fish are usually returned to the river or lake after being caught and their brains are not sufficiently developed to feel pain'. The counter-argument disputes this. It says 'fish have the same nerve endings as mammals and therefore feel pain'.

Question 4 *a*) A counter-claim is a short statement which opposes another claim. In this argument, the counter-claim is that fishing can be boring at times. It opposes the positive views that fishing is a rewarding and relaxing pastime, that being outside in the fresh air is healthy and enjoyable and that some of the scenery around rivers, lakes and canals is stunning.

***b*)** Counter-claims are not the same as counter-arguments. A counter-argument contains a reason and a conclusion. It is a complete argument persuading people to accept a particular position. A counter-claim is merely a claim that opposes another. They are short statements which are put in arguments to be dismissed immediately.

Question 5 *a*) Four year old Bibi Gul does not believe in Santa Claus. She is a Muslim and her religion does not recognise the existence of Christmas. Consequently, she will not believe in Santa Claus.

***b*)** Counter-examples can be extremely powerful tools. A single counter-example, like the one used in a), can show that a claim is incorrect. Once we accept that Bibi Gul does not believe in Santa Claus, the claim 'all young children believe in Santa Claus' is wrong.

Unit 21 Hypothetical reasoning, value judgements & definitio

Activity 1 *Hypothetical reasoning (p97)*

Question 1 *a*) A hypothetical claim states that something will happen on condition that something else happens, or that something is true provided that something else is true. In this argument, the first sentence is a hypothetical claim. It states that something will happen 'the polar icecaps will eventually melt' on condition that something else happens 'If global warming continues'.

Another hypothetical claim is made in the final sentence. It states that 'if this scenario is probable (global warming causing large cities in low-lying land to be flooded), then something must be done to halt global warming'.

b) Hypothetical claims can be used as reasons or conclusions in arguments. The first hypothetical claim in this argument is used as a reason. The claim 'if global warming continues, the polar icecaps will eventually melt' is used to support the intermediate conclusion that 'vast areas of low-lying land will be submerged under the sea…'.

The second hypothetical claim is used as the main conclusion in the argument. It states that 'if this scenario is probable (global warming causing large cities in low-lying land to be flooded), then something must be done to halt global warming'. This is the last sentence in the argument.

Question 2 Suppositional reasoning may be seen as a particular type of hypothetical reasoning. A suppositional statement usually starts with the word or phrase 'suppose' or 'what if'. Suppositional reasoning often asks a question and invites us to follow a line of reasoning in order to discover whether something has happened or whether something is true. In this argument, the author is speculating about the possible whereabouts of some lost keys as a means of finding them. For example, the author says 'Let's suppose they're in the house' and 'if we can't find them in the house let's suppose you left them at your friend's house'. This is suppositional reasoning – questions are being asked and we are invited to follow a line of reasoning. We are not being asked to believe something, just to consider 'what if'.

Activity 2 *Conflicting value judgements* (p99)

Question 1 A value judgement is a judgement based on a value. A value is a belief that something is good or bad, wrong or right, better or worse. Items B and C are both value judgements. They express different views about the large amounts of money paid to Philip Green, a wealthy businessman. Item B expresses the belief that successful business people deserve high rewards. This is because they have made important contributions to society by building efficient and productive companies and providing employment. Item C expresses a very different belief. This is that the wealth and lifestyle of people such as Philip Green are paid for by the exploitation of workers. Wealth is produced by workers whose wages are very small compared to the extremely high salaries, bonuses and dividends received by business owners.

Both these views are value judgements because they are based on ideas of right and wrong. Item B states that it is right for successful business people to receive extremely high rewards, Item C sees this as wrong.

Question 2 Two conflicting arguments are acceptable in this question. Examples of both are given here.

Philip Green does deserve the high rewards received from running Arcadia. He owns a successful business and is entitled to enjoy the profit from his risk and enterprise. He works hard and the huge financial rewards are the result of making good business decisions. If Philip Green had made poor decisions and his business suffered as a result, he may have lost a lot of money. He may also have suffered from a loss of status. His enterprise employs a lot of people who benefit from the wages paid.

This argument is based on the value judgement that entrepreneurs deserve to be rewarded for their risk and enterprise.

Philip Green deserves to be rewarded for his hard work and effort. However, £23m per week is excessive by anyone's standards! Although the success of his business is due partly to his skill and good decision-making, it could also be argued that his workforce have also made a significant contribution. There may also be external factors that have contributed to Arcadia's success, such as favourable trading conditions. Even if just 10% of the £23m per week were redistributed to the workforce, the increase in their income would be significant.

This argument is based on the value judgement that the fruits of business success should be shared more equally among the different stakeholders.

Activity 3 *Definitions (p100)*

Question 1 *a)* The definition of poverty that applies to the picture in Item A is absolute poverty. This definition states that poverty is the inability to satisfy basic human needs for food and shelter. In terms of this definition, people are considered poor if they are starving or undernourished. The picture here shows Iraqi children scavenging for food discarded by the American army in Baghdad. It illustrates absolute poverty.

b) It is important to define terms such as poverty precisely. In arguments, definitions are given to avoid vagueness, confusion and misunderstanding. Some words, such as poverty, can be defined in different ways. Because of this, such words require precise definition. Precise definitions will tend to strengthen arguments by leaving less scope for criticism.

Question 2 *a)* Item B gives two definitions of human life. The pro-life view states that human life begins as soon as a baby is conceived. The pro-choice view states that the fertilised ovum is not a human person. It has no human shape, brain or other organs and has no consciousness.

b) When presenting arguments about abortion, the definition of human life is crucial. Most people believe that killing is wrong. If people accept the pro-life definition of human life, then they would have to concede that abortion is also wrong because human life begins as soon as the baby is conceived. However, if the pro-choice definition is accepted, abortion can be accepted during the early stages of pregnancy. This is because human life has not yet begun according to their definition – abortion at this stage would not involve killing a baby.

Unit 22 Causal explanations

Activity 1 *Cause and effect (p101)*

Question

A The cause is the consumption of alcohol. The effect (the thing it causes) is a reduction in reaction speeds.

B The cause is long-distance flying and the effect is dehydration.

C The cause is unprotected sex and the effect is the spread of AIDS.

D The cause is pressure at work and the effect is a rise in stress levels.

Activity 2 *Cause, effect and explanation (p102)*

A In this argument the effect is the increase in bonuses paid to accountants in 2005. In banking and financial services, new recruits received bonuses of around 25%, up from between 10% to 15% on the previous year. The cause is the rising demand for their services in London. The increase in demand is explained by the extra work generated from new financial regulations and changes in international accounting standards.

B In this argument the effect is low educational achievement. The cause is said to be poverty. This is explained by the fact that the poor live in cramped, cold and draughty conditions and have poor diets. This leaves them tired and listless, and reduces their ability to concentrate. Children from poor family backgrounds are also likely to have part-time jobs, leaving them less time for study. Poverty often leads to ill health which can result in absence from school. And poor families are less able to afford computers, reference books and home tutors.

Activity 3 *Unit review (pp103-104)*

Question 1 The effect in this argument is the fall in university applications for the first time in six years. Applications fell by 13,000 compared to the previous year. The cause of this fall is said to be the introduction of higher tuition fees, where students will pay up to £3,000 a year towards their education. The following explanation is given. First, some students have not applied because they fear that their parents cannot afford to support them financially. Others are afraid of going into debt over the three years spent at university. Some do not want the burden of working part-time whilst studying full-time. Finally, some are confused about how much money they will actually have to pay as a result of the new fees.

Question 2 Sometimes a correlation between two things is caused by a third factor. There is no causal link between them. Instead, they just have a common cause. In this example, there is a correlation between the size of people's shoes and the size of their vocabulary. There is no causal link between these two things – shoe size doesn't affect vocabulary size, nor does vocabulary size affect shoe size. The common cause is physical maturity. As people grow, their feet become bigger and they need larger shoes. Also, as people become more mature, they develop their vocabulary and learn more words. There is no causal relationship between shoe size and vocabulary size, but both have a common cause.

Question 3 In this argument, it is claimed that a correlation exists between the level of children's aggression and the amount of time they spend watching violent TV programmes. Some researchers claim that watching violent TV programmes causes aggression in children. However, the direction of causation could be reversed. It might be argued that aggressive children prefer to watch violent TV programmes.

Question 4 *a)* It is often very difficult to establish causal relationships with any degree of certainty. Many of the causal relationships provided by science are based on laboratory experiments where it is possible to isolate variables and determine precisely the causes of specific activity. Outside the laboratory, especially where human behaviour is concerned, it is very difficult indeed to establish cause and effect. In this case, where crime rates in New York have fallen quite radically, it is difficult to say what the actual causes are. It is difficult to identify them and to measure their impact. William J Barton would claim that his zero tolerance policing was responsible for the fall in crime rates. However, as the passage indicates, zero policing was introduced in Washington DC and there was very little change in the crime rate.

b) The changing crime rates mentioned in this passage might be attributable to a multi-causal explanation. This means that there may be more than one cause for the effect mentioned. In this case, the changing crime rates in New York could have been caused by a number of factors. For example, crime rates may have fallen due to increased economic prosperity in the city. Since 1993, around 10.5 million new jobs have been created and the economy has grown steadily. Another possible cause is the decline in the crack-cocaine epidemic – a lot of crime is associated with drug use. Finally, crime may have fallen because longer prison sentences have reduced the number of criminals on the streets. Along with zero tolerance policing, all of these factors may have contributed to falling crime rates.

Unit 23 Arguments using analogy

Activity 1 Analogies (p105)

Question 1 An analogy is a comparison between two things which are seen as similar. In this picture, diseases are shown as an invading army which attacks the human body. The advancing soldiers carry banners, just like armies in earlier times, only in this case the banners identify the diseases they cause – polio, tetanus, measles, tuberculosis, whooping cough etc. They are armed with swords and spears, and supplied with ladders like those used to scale castle walls in medieval times. Some of the invaders have been killed by injections – note the syringes. However, it appears that these defences are not strong enough to repel the invading army which has overwhelmed the fallen human being.

Question 2 a) Both statements are analogies because they compare two things which are seen as similar. Money is compared to oil and genes to a collection of recipes.

b) Oil lubricates the engine and makes it run smoothly. Without oil, an engine would grind to a halt. Imagine a modern economy without money. It would have to be based on barter – the exchange of goods and services for other goods and services. For example, to fill your car with petrol, you would have to provide the owner of the petrol station with something of similar value. This might be anything from washing and ironing his family's clothes to giving him some vegetables you have grown. Today's economy is global. Imagine a worldwide system of barter. The global economy would rapidly grind to a halt, just like the engine without oil. In this respect, the analogy between money and oil helps to explain the role of money in the economy.

c) A collection of recipes provides instructions about how to make a variety of dishes – for example, beef stroganoff, shepherd's pie, chicken madras, pizza margherita, sweet and sour pork, nut roast and so on. Follow the instructions provided by the recipe and, all being well, you'll produce a tasty meal.

Comparing recipes to genes helps to explain the role of genes. Like recipes, genes contain a set of instructions. These instructions direct the body to grow and develop in particular ways. Genes instruct the growth and development of every part of the human body – from the things that make us similar – hands and feet, fingers and toes – to the things that make us distinctive – the shape of our nose and the colour of our eyes.

Genes and recipes are similar in that both provide instructions to make something. The analogy is useful to explain the role of genes to people who know little or nothing about genetics. In fact, many genetic counsellors use this analogy in discussions with their clients.

Activity 2 Analogies in arguments (p106)

Question 1 a) The argument is presented in standard form below.

R1 The metabolism of pigs is similar to that of humans.
R2 High doses of saccharine can cause cancer in pigs.

C High doses of saccharine may cause cancer in humans.

b) This argument uses an analogy between humans and pigs. An analogy is based on the idea that if two things are similar in one respect, then they are likely to be similar in other respects. In this argument, it is claimed that the metabolism of pigs is similar to the metabolism of humans. Consequently, if high doses of saccharine can cause cancer in pigs, it is likely that high doses of saccharine in humans will also cause cancer.

Medical experiments on animals are often justified by arguments based on analogy such as in this case. If pigs and humans have similar metabolisms then they are likely to be affected in the same way by heavy doses of certain chemicals. Therefore, by observing the effects on pigs of heavy doses of chemicals, scientists can predict the effects on humans with some accuracy.

Question 2 *a)* The conclusion in this argument is that animals should have similar rights to humans.

b) This argument uses an analogy between animals and humans. It is claimed that there are significant similarities between animals and humans. For example, they are both mammals that can feel pain, both communicate with each other and both are intelligent. Based on these similarities, the argument concludes that animals should have similar rights to humans. For example, they should be protected from injury and be allowed to live until they die a natural death.

Activity 3 *Unit review (p108)*

Question 1 *a)* When evaluating arguments using analogies, one of the criteria used is the number of similarities. In general, the more similarities there are, the stronger the argument. In this argument, Carl wants to lose weight and proposes to go on a diet. He compared himself to two of his friends who both lost weight on a diet. One of the similarities in this case is that Carl is going to use the same type of diet as his friends. There are many types of diet but Carl has chosen the Atkins Diet – a high-protein, high-fat, low carbohydrate diet. Another similarity in the analogy used here is that he is a similar build to his friends. People with similar builds may have similar metabolisms and their bodies may react in a similar way to types and quantities of food.

b) Another criteria used when evaluating arguments using analogies is the number of differences in the analogy. In this example two can be identified. First, Carl is not known for his will power. Going on a diet and sticking to it often takes a lot of will power. Carl's two friends had will power but, according to the passage, Carl does not. This might prevent Carl from reaching his aim. Another difference is that Carl is dieting alone. This might make it more difficult for him to lose weight. He may not have the support and encouragement to shed those pounds.

c) Another criteria used when evaluating arguments using analogies is the relevance of similarities. The relevance of similarities is in fact more important than the number of them. In this case, it is unlikely that the starting dates of the diet are relevant. Even though Carl started his diet on January 1st 2006 and his friends started on August 12th 2005, this should have no bearing on the outcome. It is not relevant.

d) The conclusion in this argument is that Carl will lose weight on the Atkins diet. The argument could be strengthened if the word 'will' was replaced by the word 'may'. Using the word 'may' makes the conclusion more cautious and therefore the argument stronger. Cautious conclusions often make stronger arguments.

Question 2 In this poem, six different blind men all describe the same thing – an elephant. However, their descriptions and conclusions are very different. For example, the first blind man likens the elephant to a wall, the second blind man likens it to a spear, the third a snake and so on. The differences in their conclusions arose because they were all describing different parts of the elephant. The poem ends by describing how, although each of the men were partly in the right, they were all in the wrong.

This poem illustrates some of the problems of using analogies in arguments. In particular, it is important that the things being compared are similar. The greater the similarity between the things being compared, the stronger the analogy and the argument which is based on it. In the poem, the blind men were not really comparing the same thing because they all explored different parts of the elephant.

Also, even when similarities are strong, the conclusions drawn from them may not be correct. In the case of the poem, all the men were comparing the same animal, yet their conclusions regarding what it actually was were all different.

Unit 24 The strengths of arguments

Activity 1 *Deductive arguments (p110)*

Question 1 *a)* A deductive argument is an argument in which the conclusion is guaranteed to follow from the reasons. If the conclusion follows with absolute certainty from the reasons, then the argument is said to be valid or deductively valid. The argument in this example is valid. The conclusion 'that a cobra is cold-blooded' is guaranteed by the reasons. There is no escaping this conclusion – it is absolutely certain. The reasoning cannot be faulted – a cobra must be cold-blooded.

b) The soundness of arguments is to do with truth. If a deductive argument is sound, then the reasons are all true and the conclusion is guaranteed to be true. In this argument both the reasons are true. All reptiles are cold-blooded and a cobra is a reptile. Therefore the argument is both valid and sound.

Question 2 *a)* This argument is valid. The conclusion is guaranteed to follow from the reasons. If all singers are American and Robbie Williams is a singer, then Robbie Williams must be American.

b) This argument is not sound. This is because the first reason is not true. Not all singers are American. We also know that Robbie Williams is British. He is not American. Even though this argument is valid, it is not sound.

Activity 2 *Inductive arguments (p111)*

Question 1 *a)* Statement A is not really relevant to this conclusion. The fact that 50 years ago, all school children had a school uniform makes little difference to the conclusion that 'school uniforms should be banned'. As a reason, it would do nothing to strengthen the argument, therefore it is not relevant.

Statement B is relevant to the conclusion. The cost of school uniforms is an issue. If some parents cannot afford to buy their children school uniforms, this would be a good reason for banning them.

Statement C is also relevant to the conclusion. If most pupils do not like wearing a uniform, this may be a reason for banning them. Their dislike of school uniforms might affect their performance at school. If they feel uncomfortable or irritated, they may not work as hard. However, many would argue that this is not a sufficient reason for banning school uniforms.

Statement D is not directly relevant to the claim made in the conclusion. The fact that school uniforms usually carry the logo or name of the school would not provide support for the banning of school uniforms. In fact, it might do the opposite. School logos or names may give pupils a sense of identity which could be a positive thing.

b) Reasons provide stronger support for a conclusion if they are based on credible evidence. In this case, the reason outlined in Statement B could be supported by evidence showing that school uniforms were more expensive than alternative clothing worn by pupils. For example, it would be easy to gather information of the cost of a blazer, jumper, trousers, shirt, school tie etc from local shops. If the cost of uniforms was compared to the cost of other clothing bought for pupils, and the comparison showed that the cost of uniforms was significantly higher, then this would support the reason.

It would also be possible to gather evidence looking at the support for a ban on uniforms amongst pupils. This could be done using a pupil survey at a school. It may also be possible to gather evidence on school uniforms and their effects on pupil performance. One way would be to compare the performances of pupils at schools where a uniform was worn with those of pupils at schools where uniforms were not worn. However, the schools would have to be carefully matched to ensure that the pupils were similar in other respects – eg, the income levels of their parents.

Question 2 *a)* The conclusion in this argument is that 'Annette probably stole the money from the safe'. This is stated in the final sentence.

b) The strength of inductive arguments depends on the probability that the conclusion is true, whether the argument contains relevant reasons, and whether there is any credible evidence to support the reasons. In this argument, one reason is that Annette is one of only two people who knew the combination of the safe. Another reason is that it was Julie who reported the money missing to the police. The evidence also points strongly to Annette's guilt. When searched by the police, Julie had £16 in her possession whilst Annette had £1,005. Further evidence was unearthed after the police interviewed the pair. It was revealed that Annette owed £11,000 on her credit cards and was scared to tell her husband. The conclusion is well supported by sound reasons and credible evidence. As a result, this is a strong argument.

Activity 3 *Unit review (p113)*

Question 1 *a)* The conclusion in this argument is that 'violence in films can lead to violence in the wider society'. This is stated in the first sentence in the argument.

b) If true, Statement A would strengthen the argument. If it could be shown that the nature of *Scream* crimes closely resembled those shown in the film, this might provide evidence that violence in films can lead to violence in the wider society.

Statement B would not strengthen the argument. Indeed, it would weaken the argument. It states that over a million people have seen *Scream* films and the overwhelming majority did not copy the violence depicted in the films. If the conclusion were true, it would be expected that more people would be influenced by what they saw in the film and therefore go on to commit violent crimes.

Statement C would not strengthen the argument either. Criminals wanting to hide their identity or frighten their victims, may well have chosen a *Scream* mask for this purpose. *Scream* masks were widely available and you did not have to watch the film to buy a mask.

Statement D might well add strength to the argument. If all the people who committed *Scream* crimes had seen a *Scream* film, this suggests that what people see in films can influence their behaviour. Consequently, violence in films might be copied and therefore the conclusion in the argument may be true.

Question 2 The quantifier in each conclusion has been changed in order to restrict it. The new quantifier is shown in bold.

A **Most** young people like pop music.

B **Nearly everybody** cleans their teeth in the morning and at night.

C Men **sometimes** drive too fast.

D **Many** women today choose not to get married.

Note Other quantifiers may be selected as alternatives to those given here.

Unit 25 Flaws in arguments 1

Activity 1 *Post hoc fallacies (p115)*

Question 1 A post hoc fallacy occurs when a conclusion does not follow from the reasoning in an argument. The fallacy is based on the mistaken idea that simply because one event happens before another, then the first event causes the second event. Such reasoning is the basis for many superstitions. The examples given here are all post hoc fallacies. There is no evidence whatsoever which shows that breaking a mirror means seven years bad luck. Nor is there any evidence to suggest that finding a four-leaf clover will bring you good luck or a black cat crossing your path brings bad luck. Superstitions like these, which suggest that one event caused the other simply because it came first, are flawed.

Question 2 The claim made in this passage is another example of a post hoc fallacy. The claim is that the more storks that nest in the city of Copenhagen, the more human babies are born. This is probably no more than a superstition although people do point to the fact that during the 12 years following World War II, the more storks that nested in Copenhagen in Spring, the more babies were born in that year. However, this correlation is probably due to coincidence. There is no evidence of a causal relationship and no explanation of how the number of nesting storks can affect the number of babies born.

Question 3 The conclusion in this argument is that the new licensing laws have resulted in a reduction in violent crime. However, the conclusion cannot be accepted because the argument is flawed. It is based on post hoc reasoning. According to the argument, a few months after the introduction of the new licensing laws, serious violent crime fell by 21%. There were also 14% fewer woundings in the same period. The argument sounds convincing but it is not. A number of other factors could have contributed to the decrease in violent crimes during that period. Examples include a fall in the detection rate, an increase in deterrents such as an increased police presence or more CCTV cameras, or a change in the way violent crime is recorded. Just because one event occurred before a second, it cannot be claimed that the first event caused the second unless credible evidence is available.

Activity 2 *Ad hominem arguments (p116)*

Question 1 *a)* Osama bin Laden claims that 'the United States has been occupying the lands of Islam in the holiest of places, the Arabian Peninsular, plundering its riches, dictating to its rulers, humiliating its people, terrorising its neighbours, and turning its bases in the peninsular into a spearhead through which to fight neighbouring Muslim peoples'. How can you believe the leader of Al Qaeda, one of the deadliest terrorist organisations in the World? He is responsible for the deaths of many thousands of innocent people such as those killed in the 9/11 terrorist attack. He has been ostracised by the world, lives in hiding and no leader on earth will welcome him into their country.

b) Ad hominem arguments are flawed. This is because they attack the author of the argument rather than the substance of the argument. Such arguments attack the reputation, honesty and credibility of the person making the argument. The argument is dismissed because the person making it has been discredited. However, these are not sufficient grounds to reject an argument. Although we must be on our guard against people who have a bad reputation, such as Osama bin Laden, we cannot automatically reject their arguments. Their arguments cannot be dismissed out of hand, with no consideration of the reasons given, the evidence they present and the conclusions they reach. For example, many people may agree with some, or all, of the claims made by Osama bin Laden.

Activity 3 *Straw man arguments (p117)*

Question 1 *a)* A straw man argument occurs when an argument is misrepresented in order to make it easier to discredit. For example, the original argument might be exaggerated, made more extreme, distorted or simplified. This weakens the argument and makes it easier to refute. In this example, Petra argues that stem cell research does not take human lives. She claims that stem cells come from surplus cells left over from in vitro fertilisation. These cells were going to die with or without research. However, Damien disagrees. He says that if we are going to experiment on things that are going to die anyway, why don't we perform experiments on old people? Damien has used a straw man argument by misrepresenting Petra's claim. He has distorted her real claim to make it an easy target to knock down. No one would agree that experimenting on old people is desirable or acceptable, but this is not what Petra said.

b) Straw man arguments are not always easy to identify, especially if you lack the subject knowledge upon which the argument is based. However, there are some features of many straw man arguments that can help you to recognise them. These include the following.

✪ Arguments that seem to be grossly exaggerated or over-simplified.

✪ Arguments which appear so obviously incorrect they could be knocked down with a feather. A person presenting a genuine argument is not likely to present such a weak argument.

✪ Arguments which contain sensational language using words such as 'wild', 'ridiculous' and 'ludicrous' to refute the original argument. Such language is often used to disguise weaknesses in arguments.

Activity 4 *Unit review (p118)*

Question 1

A This argument is based on the straw man fallacy. The claim made by the MP has been exaggerated quite significantly. The claim is that the education budget should be cut by 2%. This would not result in the closure of half the schools in the country as suggested by the author of the argument. Few, if any, people would support a cut in the education budget that would result in such a damaging effect on the country's schools. But this is not what the MP is suggesting. The author has presented a straw man which is a target to be knocked down. Therefore the argument is flawed.

B This argument is based on the tu quoque fallacy. This fallacy occurs when a person's claim is seen to be at fault because it is inconsistent with their actions or with previous claims that they have made. In this case, the argument is flawed because it rejects the original argument on the grounds that the father's advice is contrary to his actions. Father is recommending that the son or daughter goes on a diet to maintain a healthy heart – yet he is 22 stone and has never been on a diet himself. Although he might be setting a bad example through his actions, this does not provide sufficient grounds to reject his argument. Therefore, the argument is flawed.

C This argument is based on the post hoc fallacy. The author believes that if they wear a blue hat to the match their team will win. This is based on the fact that the last time the blue hat was worn their team did win. However, this is not sufficient grounds to draw the conclusion. Just because one event precedes another, it does not necessarily mean that the first event caused the second event. There is no evidence whatsoever that the wearing of a blue hat could affect the performance of a sports team. The claim in the author's argument is based on the post hoc fallacy and is therefore flawed.

D This argument is based on the ad hominem fallacy. The argument attacks the authors of the original argument on the grounds that they are fanatics and lawbreakers. However, the reputation of an author is not sufficient to dismiss their argument. One must look at the reasons, the credibility of evidence and the plausibility of a conclusion in order to dismiss it. Therefore the argument in this case is flawed.

Unit 26 Flaws in arguments 2

Activity 1 *Overgeneralisation and slippery slopes (p120)*

Question 1 *a)* Generalisations are general statements about categories of things. All of the arguments in this question contain generalisations. They are shown below.

A The vast majority of people do not regard fishing as a cruel sport.
B Women are safer drivers than men.
C The French are rude and arrogant.

b) An overgeneralisation is made when a generalisation is not supported by adequate evidence. Some of the generalisations made in these three arguments may be overgeneralisations. An analysis of the arguments is given below.

A To begin with, the evidence to support the statement 'the vast majority of people do not regard fishing as a cruel sport' looks convincing. According to the survey carried out, 98% of respondents agreed with this claim. This is a huge majority. However, the survey was not representative. It was carried out by questioning 8,000 readers of an angling magazine. It is not surprising that anglers do not think their sport is cruel. It is in their interests to say so. Although 8,000 is a large sample, the sample does not reflect people in general and therefore the evidence to support the claim is not adequate and the conclusion is very probably an overgeneralisation.

B This generalisation may be true. If the statistics provided by the insurance companies are to be believed – and there is no reason to disbelieve them – then women are safer drivers than men. The acid test would be the size of premiums paid by men and women for their car insurance. If women pay lower premiums than men this would suggest that they are safer drivers and less likely to have an accident. Car insurance premiums are linked directly to the likelihood of a claim being made. If women have fewer accidents and make fewer claims, their premiums will be lower and this would prove that women are safer drivers.

C This argument is based on a preposterous overgeneralisation. The personalities of a whole nation, 60m people, cannot be judged on the basis of a meeting with just two of them. The sample is far too small. There is insufficient evidence in this argument to support the conclusion.

Question 2 *a)* A slippery slope argument states that once the first step is taken, it leads, often inevitably, to further steps and to increasingly undesirable consequences. This argument is a slippery slope argument because it is suggesting that a bet on the Grand National can ultimately result in losing all your money and ending up on the streets as a beggar.

b) Many, but not all, slippery slope arguments are flawed. In this case, some people may follow a slippery slope into gambling, starting with a single bet on the Grand National and graduating to addictive sessions on the Internet playing poker. However, most people do not. Millions of people have a bet on the Grand National and the overwhelming majority do not end up being addicted to gambling. Most people are capable of enjoying a 'flutter' on events like the Grand National and are able to resist the temptation to take this leisure activity any further. They do not slip further down the slope and therefore this argument is flawed.

Activity 2 *Unit review (p122)*

Question 1 This argument contains an overgeneralisation. The evidence to support the generalisation that 'Stella is the UK's favourite beer' is inadequate. Just because most people in one single pub drink Stella, this is not sufficient grounds to suggest that Stella is the UK's favourite beer. There are more than 60,000 pubs in the UK. Drinking preferences in just one pub are not likely to reflect the preferences of a whole nation. The argument is therefore flawed.

Question 2 In this argument it is suggested that someone who likes to keep their house spotless will end up with no friends, divorced and diagnosed with having an obsessive compulsive disorder (OCD). This is a slippery slope argument. The author is saying that the person in the argument has taken the first step down the slippery slope by keeping the house spotless. According to the author, it is inevitable that they will graduate to spending all their time dusting, polishing, vacuuming, cleaning windows, toilets, baths and tiles and searching for cobwebs with a feather duster until eventually they are diagnosed with OCD. However, this argument is flawed because there is no evidence to suggest that everyone who likes to keep their house spotless ends up 'at the bottom of the slope' with OCD.

Question 3

A This statement is **true**. Being a female is a necessary condition for becoming pregnant. However, it is not a sufficient condition because further conditions need to be satisfied. For example, a female's eggs need to be fertilised in some way.

B This statement is **false**. Having three sides is not a sufficient condition for an equilateral triangle. It is a necessary condition but not a sufficient condition. Other conditions have to be met. For example, the three sides must be of the same length.

C This statement is **true**. Clouds are a necessary but not a sufficient condition for a rainy day. It is common to have a cloudy day without any rain.

Question 4 A circular argument is one where the reason and the conclusion are the same. In this example, the conclusion in the argument is that 'there must be a God because the Bible says so'. However, the reason says the same but using slightly different words. The reason given in the argument is that 'the Bible is the word of God'. This is a circular argument because the reason and the conclusion say the same thing.

Question 5 *a)* Arguments are flawed if they restrict or limit the options that are available. This argument restricts the options to just two. It suggests that there are only two solutions to the problem of poverty – creating jobs and ensuring that the poor apply for them. There may be other solutions to poverty. Some of these are outlined in b).

b) Some examples of solutions to poverty are outlined below.

- ✪ Redistribute national income in favour of the poor using the tax and benefit system.
- ✪ Improve educational opportunities for the poor.
- ✪ Improve training facilities for the poor.
- ✪ Improve health care for the poor.
- ✪ Provide more information for the poor about job opportunities.

Question 6 *a)* The conclusion in this argument is that 'Everybody should have a religion'. It is the first sentence in the argument.

b) An argument is inconsistent if claims within the argument contradict each other. At the end of this argument the claim is made that 'there is some truth to the view that atheists can also have purpose and direction in life'. This claim contradicts the conclusion which states that 'Everybody should have a religion' to provide them with purpose and direction. Atheists reject the belief in God or any other supernatural being. This contradiction makes the argument inconsistent and therefore it is flawed.

Unit 27 Flaws in arguments 3

Activity 1 *Unit review (p125)*

Question 1 *a)* This argument contains an appeal to authority. It implies that Gillian's views should be given credibility because she is an authority on economics and she holds a position of authority as a Justice of the Peace.

b) The appeal to authority in this argument is irrelevant because Gillian is not a qualified paediatrician – paediatrics is the branch of medicine dealing with children. Gillian holds a position of authority as a Justice of the Peace. There is no evidence in the argument to suggest that she has any specialist knowledge about the causes of cot deaths. Such knowledge is outside her field of expertise which is economics. In this case, the appeal to authority is irrelevant. The argument is therefore flawed.

Question 2

a) This advert is an appeal to pity. Such appeals are commonly used to persuade people to donate to charity. In this case, a request for donations of £3 a month is being made by ChildLine. It appeals to our pity for children who have no one to turn to. The advert also appeals to people's generosity.

b) This advert is making an appeal to novelty. Appeals to novelty are based on the idea that new equals better. The product being advertised is a new type of make-up which is said to be age defying. The advert also appeals to vanity. It attempts to persuade people that the product will improve their looks and make them appear younger.

c) This advert appeals to pity. It hopes to persuade people to make a donation to the RSPCA to prevent cruelty to animals. The advert also appeals to people's generosity. The image used in the advert may be seen as 'cute' and this could persuade some people to make a donation. In this respect, there is also an appeal to cuteness.

d) This advert is an appeal to authority. It carries an endorsement from Jeanette Brakewell. She is one of Britain's top event riders and has won medals in European and World Championships. In this case, her field of expertise is relevant and, as a result, people may be persuaded to buy the product.

e) This advert is making an appeal to fear. People are increasingly worried about their health and many want to live healthier lifestyles. This advert is promoting a product that allegedly controls blood pressure and helps to maintain a healthy heart. The advert also appeals to novelty – the product is 'new' which implies a breakthrough .

f) This advert is making an appeal to popularity. Arguments appealing to popularity attempt to persuade people that their claims are true because they have popular support. In this case, the BT offer has already been taken up by 14.6 million homes. This is a large number of people and other consumers may be persuaded to take up the offer simply because so many people already have.

Unit 28 Statistical and numerical evidence 1

Activity 1 *Bar charts (p128)*

Question 1 The parallel bar charts shown in Figure 6 provide good support for the argument. The conclusion in the argument is that parents should monitor more closely the sites visited by their children on the Internet. This is because many sites are unsuitable for children. The bar chart shows what 9-15 year olds have done on the Internet and what their parents think they have done. For example, about 70% of children have visited a chat room. This compares with parents' perceptions of just 30%. And over 40% of children have seen pornography on the Internet, compared with parents' perceptions of only 15%. Children are obviously visiting unsuitable Internet sites far more than their parents imagine. Therefore, the conclusion in the argument is one that many would accept because it is strongly supported by the statistical evidence.

Question 2 The percentage bar chart shown in Figure 7 provides good support for the argument. The conclusion in the argument is that the government must move away from landfill sites as a method of waste disposal. This is because of the many problems associated with landfill sites such as pollution and wasted resources. The bar chart shows that this can be done. It shows that other European countries make much greater use of other methods of waste disposal. For example, Denmark and the Netherlands make hardly any use of landfill – less than 5%. They rely more on recycling and incineration. In comparison, the UK dump more than 70% of their waste in landfill sites. Figure 7 provides strong evidence to support the claim in the argument that evidence from Europe shows that it is possible to move away from landfill sites for waste disposal.

Activity 2 Line graphs, pie charts and tables (pp130-131)

Question 1 The conclusion in the argument states that it is a good time to buy shares in technology companies. The data in Figure 10 supports this view. Figure 10 shows the performance of share prices in three technology companies over the last couple of years. In each case, the line graph, which represents movements in share prices, shows quite sharp increases. For example, the price of Google shares has risen from about $100 to nearly $500 over the time period. This is a significant increase and provides support for the conclusion in the argument. However, it must be remembered that the past performance of share prices is not necessarily a good guide to future performance. Most investors understand this.

Question 2 The conclusion in the argument states that the introduction of tuition fees is likely to result in a fall in university applications. This is because university students are increasingly finding it difficult to make ends meet. The pie charts in Figure 11 show the composition of student income in 1998/99 and 2002/03. There are some significant changes. Government grants have been completely abolished as a source of income. There has been a significant increase in the amount of money borrowed by students in the form of student loans and the amount of income from employment has increased. The proportion of income contributed by parents has also fallen slightly. This evidence shows that the financial pressure on students has increased since they lost government grants and had to borrow more and work more. The evidence in Figure 11 strengthens the argument that the introduction of tuition fees will place further financial pressures on students and may well put more people off from applying to university.

Question 3 The conclusion in this argument is that women are having children at an older age than they were 30 years ago. The evidence provided in Table 2 supports this claim. For example, the average age of a mother having a first child has risen from 23.7 years in 1971 to 27.1 years in 2004. Looking at the figures for all births, the increase in age is less significant. The average age of mothers for all births has risen from 26.6 in 1971 to 28.9 in 2004. This evidence supports the conclusion in the argument.

Activity 3 Unit review (pp132-133)

Question 1 The conclusion in this argument is that fewer IT staff are likely to be needed in the future. The bar chart in Figure 13 shows the number of IT vacancies in the UK between 2001 and 2005. The information in this chart supports the conclusion. It shows that IT vacancies have fallen from about 375,000 in 2001 to around 150,000 in 2005. However, if we start from the middle of 2003, there has been a slow but steady rise in IT vacancies, followed by a 5% decline in the first quarter of 2005. If the overall trend from mid-2003 continues, then there will be a further small rise in IT vacancies. This contradicts the conclusion that fewer IT vacancies will be needed in the future. Figure 13 therefore provides evidence both for and against the conclusion.

Question 2 *a)* The main conclusion in this argument is that the BBC needs to be regulated more tightly by the government.

b) (i) Some of the information in Figure 14 adds weight to the argument. For example, the BBC has the sixth most popular website in the UK. In January 2006, it had an audience of 12,141,000. This suggests that the BBC is very prominent in this market and supports the conclusion. Figure 14 also shows that the BBC's share of the radio market is growing. Between 1999 and 2005, the BBC's share of the radio market increased from around 50% to nearly 55%. This might also add weight to the argument calling for tighter control over the BBC.

(ii) Despite the statistical support for tighter control over the BBC shown in Figure 14, there is also some evidence which suggests the BBC is not quite as powerful as it used to be. The line graph in the middle of the three images shows a fall in the BBC's share of TV audiences. For example, BBC 1's share has fallen from nearly 40% to under 30%. This is quite a sharp fall and some would say it is particularly significant since the BBC's core business is television broadcasting. This statistical evidence might weaken the argument considerably.

Question 3 *a)* Extend the vertical axis and/or reduce the horizontal axis. The example shown here reduces the horizontal axis by 50% relative to the vertical axis.

b) People who are campaigning against gun crime would want to show that gun crime is rising rapidly. The gee-whiz graph drawn in a) appears to shows a much steeper increase in gun crime. This may add weight to their campaign because the graph may help to convince others that gun crime is rising at a drastic rate.

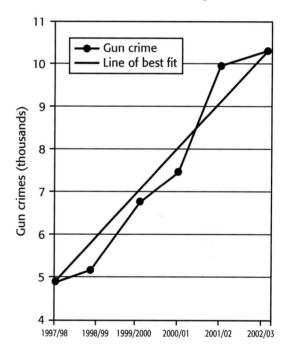

Total crimes involving firearms

Unit 29 Statistical and numerical evidence 2

Activity 1 Percentages (p134)

Question 1 This argument uses percentages to show that ethnic minorities are more entrepreneurial than White British people. According to the numerical evidence, in 2002/03, 23% of Pakistanis and 18% of Chinese people living in Britain were self-employed. This compares with just 12% of White British people. This information could have been presented using the actual numbers of self-employed people. This is shown below.

British White 6,000,000 (12% x 50,000,000)
Pakistanis   165,140 (23% x 718,000)
Chinese   35,820 (18% x 199,000)

If the information had been presented in actual numbers, the argument does not look convincing. For example, the actual number of Pakistanis who were self-employed in 2002/03, was 165,140. This compares with a massive 6,000,000 of British White people. This outcome arises because the number of White British people living in Britain is so much higher (50 million).

Question 2 The percentage change in the number of drug offences between 1993 and 2003 is given by:

$$\frac{51,200 - 21,900}{21,900} \times 100 = \frac{29,300 \times 100}{21,900} = 133.8\%$$

b) The government should increase the penalties for drug offences. Between 1993 and 2003 there was a large increase in drug offences in the UK. Evidence shows that offences increased by 133.8%, ie they have more than doubled in just 10 years.

Activity 2 *Unit review (p138)*

Question 1 In this argument, the conclusion is that the government should open more NHS Walk-in Centres due to their growing popularity. According to the statistical evidence, the mean number of daily visits has increased from 30 to 103 in 4 years. The mean can be a very useful measure. This is because the mean is an average number and can reflect a whole set of data. In this case, the mean number reflects the average daily number of visits over a whole year. An alternative approach would have been to compare the actual number of visits on a particular day in each of the two years 2000 and 2004. However, such a comparison might not reflect the whole data set because, on the particular day chosen for comparison, there could have been an untypical number of visits to Walk-in Centres. The mean is very useful for making comparisons between data in this way since untypical data are removed from the comparison.

Question 2 In this argument, the conclusion is that you should think twice about hiring a car in Portugal. This is because the risk of being killed in a road accident is much higher than in the UK. Evidence for this is provided by the death rates on roads in each country. In Portugal, there were 16.1 road deaths per 100,000 in 2002. In the UK, there were only 6.1 deaths per 100,000. This statistical evidence provides strong support for the argument. However, if the road deaths had been expressed in actual numbers the evidence might have looked weak. This is because in 2002, a total of 1,660 people were killed on the roads in Portugal. This compares with about 3,600 in the UK. This might have led people to conclude that driving in Portugal was safer. However, measuring the incidence of road deaths in rates takes into account the size of the population in both countries. This provides a more appropriate comparison.

Unit 30 Writing arguments

Activity 1 *Writing a simple argument (p140)*

Question 1

A Examples of reasons which might support the conclusion are listed below.

✪ Non-renewable energy sources such as oil and gas are being depleted rapidly.

✪ The price of non-renewable sources is rising rapidly.

✪ The amount of money currently being invested in renewable energy sources is small compared with the amount spent on non-renewable sources.

✪ The use of non-renewable energy sources is contributing to global warming.

The government should invest more money in renewable energy sources such as wind, solar and wave power. This is because burning non-renewable energy sources such as gas, oil and coal is making a major contribution to global warming. Non-renewable energy sources such as oil and gas are being depleted rapidly. They are in danger of running out and they cannot be replaced. In addition, the price of non-renewable resources is rising rapidly. Compared to the amount spent on non-renewable sources, the investment in renewable sources of energy is very low.

B Examples of reasons which might support the conclusion given here are listed below.

✪ Recycling household waste can reduce the use of landfill sites which are costly, unsightly, and can cause pollution.

✪ Recycling reduces the pressure on the environment, eg for wood and minerals.

✪ Recycling can provide useful products, eg paper, glass, metal and compost.

✪ Private companies may not find recycling sufficiently profitable.

✪ Since local authorities are in charge of household waste disposal, it makes sense for them to organise recycling.

Local authorities should invest more money in recycling household waste. Recycling has a number of benefits. It can reduce the use of landfill sites which are costly, unsightly, and can cause pollution. It reduces the pressure on the environment, eg for wood and minerals. And it can provide useful products, eg paper, glass, metal and compost. Local authorities are the ideal candidates to recycle household waste. Private companies may not find recycling sufficiently profitable. Since local authorities are in charge of household waste disposal, it makes sense for them to organise recycling.

Activity 2 *Arguments with evidence (p141)*

Question 1 The government's dental reforms will help to improve the provision of dental care in the UK. There will be a new fees structure aimed at making the system fairer and simpler. The old system was complex and involved around 400 different charges. Under the new system there will be just three charges – £15.50 for a check-up, £42.40 for a check-up and filling and £189 for more complex work such as crowns. The new system will also encourage more dentists to undertake NHS work which will give people greater access to dental services. This will be achieved by providing dentists with a guaranteed income of around £80,000 a year if they provide services for the local community. Under this system, dentists have to provide a set number of 'units of dental activity'. The idea is to move away from a piece-work system of payment – a situation which led to a 'drill and fill' culture, which encouraged some dentists, it is claimed, to over-treat patients to maximise their income.

Activity 3 *Arguments with intermediate conclusions (p143)*

Question 1

The argument is presented in standard form below. (EV stands for evidence.)

R1 Truancy levels have not fallen despite expenditure of nearly £1bn.

EV The truancy rate remains at 0.7% according to the National Audit Office.

IC Money spent by the government to reduce truancy has been wasted.

R2 Truancy is a serious problem.

EV Truants miss out on £1.6bn of education each year and are more prone to being drawn into undesirable activities such as crime and anti-social behaviour.

C New measures are needed to deal with the problem of truancy.

Despite expenditure of nearly £1 billion to deal with the problem of truancy, levels have not fallen. According to the National Audit Office the truancy rate has remained at 0.7%. Therefore, the money spent by the government has been wasted. Truancy is a serious problem. When pupils miss school they are not benefiting from education to the value of £1.6 billion. Truants are also likely to get drawn into undesirable activities such as crime and anti-social behaviour. Therefore, the government must introduce new measures to deal with the problem of truancy.

Activity 4 *Counter-arguments (p144)*

There are two main ways of presenting a counter-argument. One is to challenge every reason given in the opposing argument. The second is to present reasons not dealt with in the opposing argument and use them to challenge that argument. The counter-argument presented here uses the first approach. The counter-argument is presented in standard form below.

R1 There is no credible evidence to prove that capital punishment acts as a deterrent.
R2 Many people who kill do not rationally consider the consequences of their actions.
IC Capital punishment does not act as a deterrent.
R3 In a world of imperfect information, innocent individuals may be convicted and executed.
R4 Even with advances in forensic methods, such as DNA testing, mistakes can still be made.
IC2 Innocent people may still be executed.
R5 The costs of life imprisonment are small compared to the execution of innocent people.

C   Capital punishment cannot be justified.

Capital punishment does not act as a deterrent for murder. There is no credible evidence which proves that capital punishment discourages people from committing murder. Also, many people who commit murder do not rationally consider the consequences of their actions.

If capital punishment was reintroduced there is still a danger that innocent people might be executed. In a world of imperfect information, innocent people may be convicted and executed before information showing their innocence comes to light. There is also the danger that mistakes might be made with forensic evidence. Even with developments in science and technology, such as DNA testing, mistakes are still possible and innocent people could be executed.

Finally, the costs of life imprisonment are small compared to the execution of innocent people. Therefore, capital punishment should not be reintroduced for any crime.

Another counter-argument using the second approach is presented in standard form below. It uses human rights issues to challenge the opposing argument.

R1 Life is a basic human right.
R2 The method of execution can be painful and is therefore a form of torture.
R3 Keeping people on Death Row for many years is a form of torture.
IC Capital punishment denies basic human rights.

C Capital punishment should not be reintroduced.

Activity 5 *Arguments using hypothetical reasoning (p145)*

Question

It is now 2014. It is looking increasingly likely that the asteroid will hit the Earth in 2028. Here is a hypothetical argument suggesting some of the possible negative effects of this growing threat to Earth.

For many people, hedonism – pleasure seeking – has replaced the work ethic. What's the point of working when the world may be coming to an end? The consumption of hard drugs and alcohol is rocketing. Prostitutes are doing a roaring trade. Clubs are full to bursting point.

Public services, such as transport and the health service, are on the verge of collapse with increasing numbers of employees failing to turn up for work.

Some people appear to have lost the will to live. Life seems pointless. This is reflected in the rapidly rising suicide rate.

Others are looking for salvation in religion. New religions have sprung up around the world offering an afterlife of eternal happiness after the asteroid hits Earth.

In some areas, law and order has broken down as people rob and steal to fund their cravings for drugs, sex and a variety of other pleasures.